Japanese Home Cooking

Quick, easy, delicious recipes to make at home

The Essential Asian Kitchen

Japanese Home Cooking

SHUNSUKE FUKUSHIMA

PERIPLUS

First published in the United States in 2001 by Periplus Editions (HK) Ltd.,
with editorial offices at 153 Milk Street, Boston, Massachusetts 02109
and 130 Joo Seng Road #06-01/03 Olivine Building Singapore 368357

© Copyright 2001 Lansdowne Publishing Pty Ltd

Library of Congress Cataloging-in-Publication Data is available.
ISBN 0-7946-5003-1

DISTRIBUTED BY

North America
Tuttle Publishing
Distribution Center
Airport Industrial Park
364 Innovation Drive
North Clarendon, VT 05759-9436
Tel: (802) 773-8930
Tel: (800) 526-2778

Japan and Korea
Tuttle Publishing
RK Building, 2nd Floor
2-13-10 Shimo-Meguro,
Meguro-Ku
Tokyo 153 0064
Tel: (03) 5437-0171
Fax: (03) 5437-0755

Asia Pacific
Berkeley Books Pte. Ltd.
130 Joo Seng Road
#06-01/03
Olivine Building
Singapore 368357
Tel: (65) 280-3320
Fax: (65) 280-6290

Commissioned by Deborah Nixon
Recipes: Carol and Shunsuke Fukushima
Introduction text: Angus Cameron
Photographer: Louise Lister
Stylist: Suzie Smith
Designer: Robyn Latimer
Editor: Judith Dunham
Production Manager: Sally Stokes
Project Co-ordinator: Alexandra Nahlous

First Edition
06 05 04 03 02 01   10 9 8 7 6 5 4 3 2 1

Set in Spartan Classified on QuarkXPress
Printed in Singapore

Contents

Introduction

My first memory of a cooking lesson is as a very young boy hanging around my mother in the family kitchen as she made our meals and watching the different techniques that she utilized with such grace and ease. Every meal was wonderful and so it was only natural that when I opened my first restaurant, my mother's ideas and inspiration were instrumental to the meal creations.

Japanese cuisine is not difficult. This book will give the home cook a wonderful guide to a variety of recipes and dishes that will enable them to create Japanese cuisine easily and experiment with their own elegant and graceful creations.

The recipes in this book demonstrate the simplicity of Japanese cooking at home, in both its preparation and its presentation. The elaborate dishes you've eaten in restaurants are not what the average Japanese comes home to each day. On the contrary, they're meant to impress in a restaurant setting. They're the result of years of training at academies throughout Japan, where budding chefs are schooled, among other things, in the traditions, techniques and intricacies of presentation. Whether you aspire to match such displays is up to you. The point is that Japanese food, which is intended to appeal to the eye as much as to the palate, can impress in less elaborate but no less enticing forms in your own home.

History and geography

Japan consists of four main islands, Honshu, Hokkaido, Shikoku and Kyushu, and thousands of smaller islands, with a climate ranging from subarctic in the north to subtropical in the south. A mountainous country, it is also one of the world's most volcanically active. Despite lush forests and heavy rainfall, just sixteen percent of the land area is under agriculture, predominantly rice farming, a tradition inherited from China around 300 B.C. It is hardly surprising, then, that rice has become a venerated staple in Japan and that the produce of the seas surrounding the islands plays such a significant role in the nutrition of its 125 million inhabitants.

The ancestors of the Japanese came from China via what is now Korea, and between the sixth and the eighth centuries A.D., Japanese culture borrowed, adapted and developed its unique identity from China's models. Chinese ideograms became the foundation of the written language. Buddhist monks brought their frugal religion, martial arts, chopsticks, soy beans and tea. Chinese music was heard in Japanese courts, while Chinese art, architecture and pottery also made their mark. Even the Japanese name for the country, "Nippon," came from the Chinese "tai nyih pung kok," meaning "great sunrise kingdom." We owe it to Marco Polo, who transcribed the Chinese name as chipango, that we now call it Japan.

Culinary history

Early Japan, with its natural shortage of raw materials, was unable to replicate the rich variety of Chinese cuisine. When free contact with China came to an end around A.D. 790, with the collapse of the T'ang Dynasty in China and the birth of the Heian period in Japan, a golden age of Japanese culture dawned. Elaborate codes of etiquette were developed to govern almost all aspects of social life, including the presentation of food, which remained simple and natural, though abundant.

When the samurai came to power during the Kamakura period (1185–1333), a new food tradition evolved which modified the formal rituals practiced by the nobility. Feudal warlords, the samurai in the fourteenth and fifteenth centuries introduced their own food culture, "kaiseki," from the Chinese term for "meeting place." Whereas the cuisine of the ruling military class had been characterized by vast quantities of food arranged amid great ornamentation, kaiseki did away with dishes arrayed merely to be admired, omitted cold dishes and substituted food of high quality brought to the table and intended to be eaten immediately. Cold dishes later reappeared and were eaten as they arrived—chilled.

The kaiseki food tradition is inextricably linked to tea drinking and the evolution of the tea ceremony. Brick tea had come to Japan from China during the eighth or ninth century, when it became a short-lived fad among the ruling elite. It was not until the late eleventh century that powdered green tea and the tea ceremony became part of Japanese culture. At first, only sweetmeats were served before the tea at simple gatherings called chakai, but the sixteenth century saw the emergence of cha kaiseki (a forerunner of Western nouvelle cuisine and cuisine minceur), food to be served at chaji, the full tea ceremony. In accordance with Zen frugality, this food, prepared as simply as possible so that its natural taste was not disguised, was served before the tea but in quantities that left the diner room to appreciate the tea that followed.

Regionalism

National cuisines invariably develop regional specialties and Japanese cuisine is no exception. Although modern methods of transport mean that regional ingredients can be purchased in season all over Japan, cooking methods and an emphasis on particular foods persist. This is the case on the southern island of Okinawa. The flavors of Okinawan dishes tend to be stronger and spicier than in traditional Japanese cuisine, with pronounced Chinese influences. As in China, pork is a major ingredient, with every part of the pig being used. Local seafood figures prominently, as do tropical fruits and vegetables. Black sugar and awamori, a brandylike rice liqueur, are used in cooking.

On the Noto Peninsula of western Honshu, seasonal dishes include wild oysters in July, sweet shrimp (prawns) in autumn and winter, and local matsutake mushrooms from the mountains of Noto and Yamashiro in October and November. Winter yellowtail for sashimi arrive in December in the ports of Nanao and Ushitsu on the Sea of Japan, as they have for the past 400 years.

Chanpon is a famous local specialty of Nagasaki on the island of Kyushu. It consists of pork, squid, shrimp (prawns), oysters and fish fried in lard with vegetables and served in a bowl of Chinese noodles and a soup made from pork and chicken. In Hakusan, also in western Honshu, May is the season for families to venture into the mountains of Ishikawa in search of mountain vegetables, brackens and ferns.

Tea ceremony

Chanoyu, the Japanese tea ceremony, was originally a Buddhist ritual introduced to Japan from China in the eleventh century. It was thought by the Buddhist monks that green tea, which has a high caffeine content, was more conducive to enlightenment than extended periods of meditation. The rituals associated with the ceremony became increasingly elaborate and, by the fifteenth and sixteenth centuries, had developed into an art form at the Imperial Court. Tea masters dictated the number of people to be present, the positions of vessels and implements, and the architecture and decoration of the tea room. These rituals persist today, with the tea ceremony, though still formally practiced in Zen temples, an important social activity in Japanese society generally.

At the start of the ceremony, which can last several hours if it is part of an elaborate meal, a silk cloth (fukusa) is used to clean the spoon, tea container and bowl. The bowl is then washed in hot water before the tea is added with a long bamboo spoon. Hot but not boiling water is poured over the tea powder, which is then whisked until a froth forms. The bowl is passed graciously and with formal gestures to the drinker to savor.

Modern Japanese food

Increasing contact with the West and the growth of in- and outward-bound tourism have seen the Japanese accept foreign cuisines or modify traditional dishes to incorporate foreign influences. Food fashions come and go, but French, Italian, Chinese and Korean menus remain favorites. Hamburgers and American-style fast foods are popular among the young.

Two words describe the broad categories of food available today in Japan. "Washoku" refers to traditional Japanese food or meals, "wa" meaning "Japanese-style" and "shoku" meaning "food." Washoku meals continue to be served in an array of small dishes, beautifully presented and with a concentration on seafood. "Yoshoku" refers to non-Japanese foods, "yo" meaning "Western-style." Chinese foods, called "chuka," are often presented in the Japanese style and are a popular form of home cooking. They tend to be an adaptation of the Chinese original, with ramen noodles, for example, which originated in China, being especially popular cooked in a variety of soup stocks.

In the home, basic, simple food reigns. Modern Japanese are moving away from the traditional breakfast of rice, miso and side dishes to

Japanese-style breads. For lunch, the bento box, especially if it contains onigiri (filled rice balls) is popular, as are thin-crust pizzas or pastas. A typical evening meal will consist of rice and miso soup, a main dish and several side dishes, perhaps a vegetable, a salad or pickles. The Japanese believe that you should eat around thirty different kinds of food each day—easy enough as many Japanese dishes require four or more ingredients.

Meal components are served in small, individual dishes for each person, with the food prepared in a way that preserves its original color, texture and appearance. Seasonal changes are reflected in the tableware used, the choice of ingredients and the method of cooking. Chopsticks, their shape an elegant adaptation of the Chinese version, are used, as is Western-style cutlery, depending on the type of food being eaten.

Meat

Although birds and poultry had earlier been part of the Japanese diet, pork and beef appeared only over the past 150 years, when Japan opened its doors to the West. Introduced by Portuguese and Dutch explorers and missionaries, meat had previously been scorned by the Japanese as a Western peculiarity, but its consumption gradually spread inland from the coastal trading ports. Nowadays, beef, especially, is greatly prized and very expensive. Kobe beef stands out above all other varieties for its fine marbling, the result of careful pampering throughout the animal's life, and is widely considered to be the best in the world.

Tempura

One of the West's enduring food legacies to Japan is the tempura method of deep-frying seafood and vegetables. Introduced by the Portuguese in the sixteenth century, it is thought to be named after the Portuguese word "temporas" (Lent) and to be based on the Catholic practice of deep-frying fish on Fridays. By the late nineteenth century, tempura had become Japan's favorite fast food. Today, there are no foreign associations with tempura, which has become synonymous throughout the world with Japanese cuisine.

The staple fare of Japan, however, is still rice and fish, with shoyu (soy sauce). Traditional Japanese cuisine continues to lean heavily toward seafood, but vegetable dishes are popular too, as are vegetarian meals. Food is commonly prepared using boiling water or soup stock,

by poaching, simmering or blanching. Country-style meals favor the inclusion of pickles, which are usually eaten in small quantities as accompaniments. The healthiness of Japanese cooking generally is attested by the low quantities of fat and oils used in its preparation. Salt is not used much, other than in miso or soy sauce, and soup stocks are nearly fat free.

Sushi and sashimi

Fish and other forms of seafood are regarded as good for the health, and we have the Japanese to thank for exporting sushi and sashimi. Sushi comes in two main forms: nigiri-zushi and maki-zushi. Thought to have originated in Edo (the former name for Tokyo), nigiri-zushi consists of a bite-sized ball of vinegared rice spread with a little wasabi and topped with a piece of thinly sliced seafood. Fish and squid are served raw, while octopus and shrimp (prawns) are cooked. A piece of omelette may also form the topping, as can salmon roe or sea urchin held in place with a strip of nori.

Maki-zushi is named for the makisu, the bamboo mat used to roll these sushi. Vinegared rice is spread on a sheet of nori and topped with a variety of ingredients, including tuna, crab meat, ginger, shredded omelette, tofu or cucumber. Maki-zushi tends to be less expensive than nigiri-zushi as less seafood goes into its composition.

Sashimi is merely thinly sliced seafood without the rice. In accordance with the Japanese belief that seafood should be eaten fresh and raw, all but octopus, which is boiled first, are served that way. Because they cannot be sliced, oysters are not considered sashimi. The preparation of some sashimi requires the skill and experience of a trained chef, especially in the care of the high-quality, one-sided knives used. Sashimi is normally eaten at the start of a meal, accompanied by a dipping sauce of wasabi and soy.

Teppanyaki

Teppanyaki is a form of Japanese cooking that is becoming increasingly popular in Western countries, especially the United States. Literally, the word means food "grilled on a hot iron plate." A distinction must be made, however, between the kind of teppanyaki dining experience enjoyed in Japan and its Western counterpart.

It has been suggested that the teppanyaki style of cooking was created in the eighteenth century by Japanese migrants to the United States. Faced with kitchens quite different from those they were accustomed to in Japan, they adopted the grill as a means of quickly preparing fresh food in season with a minimum of cooking.

While there is no question that teppanyaki cooking produces a typically healthy Japanese meal, its popularity in the West owes much to the performance of the chef preparing the meal. In Japan, the chef simply prepares and serves the food. In the West, the cooking procedure is as much a piece of theater as food preparation, sometimes more so. In addition to scooping and tossing the ingredients flamboyantly about a large, flat grill plate to the delight of waiting diners, Western-style teppanyaki chefs specialize in juggling their cooking implements. Nothing brings greater applause at the end of the cooking than a sharp knife or cleaver being flipped into the air and caught in the chef's toque.

Serving Japanese food

It is a given in Japan that food should appeal as much to the eyes as to the palate. And it is the enormous variety of serving and eating utensils available in Japan that changes the humblest meal into a dining experience. Whereas in Western cultures cutlery and tableware usually come in matching sets, this is not generally the case in Japan, where each utensil may have a different texture, pattern or seasonal use and color. So it is preferable to invest in beautiful tableware rather than in a wide range of utensils.

Japanese-style tableware, especially square and rectangular plates, and any number of small soup and garnish bowls are readily available in Asian markets and specialty stores, so it is possible to assemble a visually appealing array of containers. Diners are usually presented with a series of small dishes, with rice or communal dishes such as sukiyaki being served in the center of the table for diners to help themselves or to be served by the host. For that extra Japanese touch, try to ensure that you present each diner with an odd number of dishes, as odd numbers are regarded as positive in the yin–yang system. If serving sake, heat in a pitcher (tokkuri) and serve in tiny china cups (sakazuki).

Japanese chopsticks have longer and more pointed ends than the Chinese variety. Those used at home and in restaurants are usually made of lacquered wood or bamboo. Disposable chopsticks are the norm in less expensive restaurants or with bento boxes. Using chopsticks, which takes practice, ensures that food must be served in manageable, bite-sized pieces. Chopsticks are readily available in a variety of finishes from Asian markets.

In Japan, the order and number of courses varies between home and restaurant. At lunchtime, the bento box is a preferable alternative to fast food. At formal meals in the West, the standard procedure is to begin with starters or appetizers, followed by the main dish, then dessert. The Japanese approach is similar, but based on a sequence of light food, heavy food, and then rice. Rice and soup or fresh fish, for example, may be followed by a grilled dish, a simmered dish, pickles to refresh the palate, a deep-fried dish, light pickles and rice. Sake connoisseurs follow a similar pattern: dry sake, sweet sake, and then dry sake, accompanied by a series of light dishes. When treating guests to a Japanese meal at home, rather than trying to emulate the intricacies of a kaiseki restaurant meal, opt instead to serve all the dishes at once and in small quantities. It is perfectly acceptable for your guests to ask for second helpings of rice and soup, and to sip sake between dishes, except after the final rice dish. Finish with green tea and prepared fresh fruit.

Etiquette do's and don'ts

Do say itadakimasu (literally, "I will eat/drink") before the meal and gochiso-sama ("everything was delicious") after the meal.

Do lift bowls of rice or soup toward you to eat the contents. This prevents you from dropping food and, in the case of soup, allows you to drink it directly from the bowl.

Do slurp your noodles.

Do dip sushi in the accompanying sauce using your fingers or chopsticks.

Do accept a second helping of rice or soup with both hands and place it on the tray or table before beginning to eat from it.

Do follow a morsel from a dish with a mouthful of rice.

Do place your chopsticks on the chopstick rest when not using them.

Don't start eating until everyone has been served.

Don't use your chopsticks to shift dishes.

Don't point with your chopsticks or wave them in the air.

Don't pick over the food with your chopsticks looking for tasty items.

Don't spear food with the points of your chopsticks.

Don't pick up a dish with the hand holding the chopsticks.

Don't leave your chopsticks standing vertically in the rice.

Equipment

The small kitchens prevalent in modern Japan and the ready availability of many prepared ingredients mean that few special utensils are required to produce traditional Japanese food. The essentials are a rice maker, a sharp knife, a chopping board, Japanese chopsticks (hashi have pointed ends, while the Chinese variety are blunt), a bamboo mat (makisu) for rolling sushi, and a Japanese mandoline (oroshigane) for grating and slicing just about anything.

1. Bamboo rolling mat

Bowls and equipment

2. Square sauce bowls
3. Stainless steel mixing bowls
4. Portable gas stove top
5. Chopsticks
6. Fan (uchiwa)

Graters

7. Porcelain grater
8. Steel grater

Knives and cutting equipment

9. Cleavers, 1 large and 1 small
10. Knives, carving
11. Knife, heavy duty
12. Knife, sashimi filleting
13. Knife, vegetable
14. Vegetable cutters
15. Wooden cutting boards

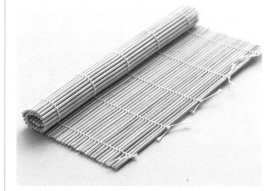

1. Bamboo rolling mat

2. Square sauce bowls

3. Stainless steel mixing bowls

4. Portable gas stove top

5. Chopsticks

6. Fan

7. Porcelain grater

8. Steel grater

9. Cleavers

10. Knives, carving

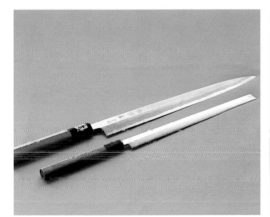

11. Knife, heavy duty

12. Knife, sashimi filleting

13. Knife, vegetable

14. Vegetable cutters

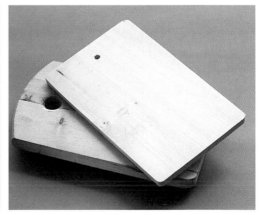

15. Wooden cutting boards

Pans

1. Frying pan, large
2. Square omelette pan

Peelers and implements

3. Peelers
4. Mandoline
5. Scaler
6. Tweezers

Pots and cookers

7. Bamboo steamer
8. Japanese donabe
   (earthenware pot, also see
   Glossary page 122)
9. Rice cooker
10. Wok

Spoons

11. Soup spoon
12. Pasta/noodle spoon
13. Strainer
14. Wire skimmer
15. Wooden rice paddle
    (shamoji)

1. Frying pan, large

2. Square omelette pan

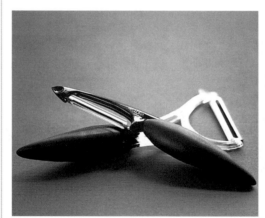

3. Peelers

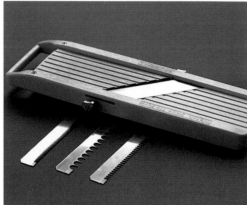

4. Mandoline

5. Scaler

6. Tweezers

7. Bamboo steamer

8. Japanese donabe

9. Rice cooker

10. Wok

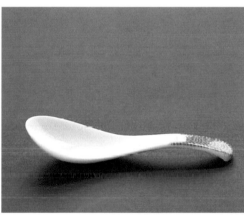

11. Soup spoon

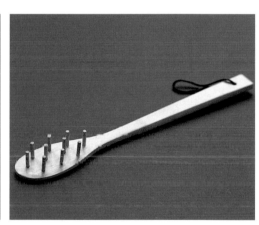

12. Pasta/noodle spoon

13. Strainer

14. Wire skimmer

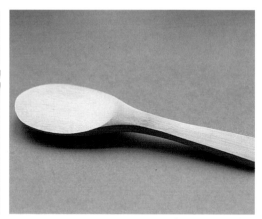

15. Wooden rice paddle (shamoji)

Japanese ingredients

In keeping with our assertion that Japanese food is not as daunting as its presentation might suggest, the list here covers those basics that will enable you to prepare all of the recipes in this book.

Aburaage and atsuage Aburaage is fried thin tofu that is normally combined with other ingredients. Atsuage is a form of tofu that comes thickly sliced and fried briefly in extremely hot oil until the surface of the slices are crisp but the interior remains soft and silken. Atsuage can be eaten on its own with ginger-flavored soy sauce or in a salad.

Azuki A red bean especially popular in Japan (see Azuki beans, page 115). It is often combined with sugar and consumed with green tea or mixed into ice cream.

Bonito flakes Flakes of dried bonito fish, rich in minerals, vitamins and proteins, used for stock. For katsuobushi shaved flakes, see page 21

Daidai Bitter orange juice that is mixed with soy sauce to make ponzu dipping sauce (see Ponzu sauce, page 119).

Daikon This giant white radish, eaten in a variety of forms as an aid to digestion, is enormously popular in Japan. It is often grated and among its many uses, it is consumed with soy sauce (see Usu-zukuri, page 41) or in a dipping sauce to accompany tempura

Aburaage

Azuki

Bonito flakes (Katsuobushi)

Daidai

Daikon

Dashi

Ginger (Shoga)

Goma

Gyoza wrappers

Hijiki

Katsuobushi

Dashi A Japanese stock, best made fresh (see Dashi, page 28). Based on dried kelp (konbu) and dried bonito (katsuobushi) flakes, dashi is also available as granules, an instant form that is fine for use in soups and broths.

Ginger Thick rootlike rhizome of the ginger plant with a sharp, pungent flavor. Once the thin tan skin is peeled from fresh ginger, the flesh is grated or sliced. Store fresh ginger in the refrigerator for 2–3 days.

Goma These sesame seeds come in three colors: black, white and golden, with the golden having the strongest aroma. The white variety is used in goma dofu (sesame tofu), a food important in Buddhist vegetarianism.

Gyoza wrappers Thin circles of dough (see Gyoza, page 99), made with eggs, used to make dumplings. Similar to Chinese gow gee or wonton wrappers.

Hijiki Rich in minerals and proteins, this black seaweed is available dried (see Seaweed salad, page 57).

Katsuobushi (bonito flakes) Dried, smoked, cured bonito fish commonly available as shaved flakes. Also sold in blocks that are shaved with a special utensil. The flakes are often used to make soup stocks or as a garnish. Available in airtight plastic bags.

Kome Although consumption of rice (kome if uncooked) is declining in Japan, the short-grained variety "Oryza sativa japonica" remains a very important food and is cooked and eaten in many forms, from gohan (boiled) to sekihan (red rice, used for celebrations).

Konbu/kombu This kelp is one of the main ingredients of dashi, itself basic to innumerable Japanese dishes. A cold-water seaweed that grows off the northern coasts of Japan, konbu is dried for sale and comes in lengths or folded. It does not need washing before use; just wipe with a damp cloth.

Matcha A bitter, caffeine-rich form of tea (see Matcha ice cream, page 112) first drunk in Japan in the ninth century A.D. This green-tea powder is associated with the traditional Japanese tea ceremony.

Mirin A very sweet, amber-colored rice wine, used as a flavoring in cooking. It can contain up to fourteen percent alcohol, but this usually evaporates during cooking.

Miso A fermented paste of soy beans, barley or rice, and salt, miso is most familiar in miso soup, but can also be used to make a sauce for grilled foods. It will keep in the refrigerator for one year.

Mustard Hot English mustard is ideal for Japanese recipes. White and brown mustard seeds are blended to make this mustard.

Kome

Konbu

Matcha

Mirin

Miso

Mustard (Karashi)

Panko

Nori

Sake

Shiitake mushrooms

Shoyu

Shungiku

Panko These dried white bread crumbs come in both fine and coarse varieties. Used to coat deep-fried foods, they tend to be crunchier than Western varieties.

Nori Dark green seaweed. Toasted nori is used mainly to wrap sushi, but also appears as finely shredded strips used for garnish.

Sake An essential accompaniment, sake or rice wine is available in a wide range of prices and flavors (from extra dry to quite sweet). It is customarily drunk warm and, with an alcohol content of around sixteen percent, is quite potent. High-quality sake is preferred at ambient temperature or chilled.

Shiitake mushrooms These are available fresh or dried. Fresh shiitake are delicious as tempura, while the dried varieties, which keep indefinitely, are more suitable for making stocks.

Shoyu Although there are six varieties of Japanese soy sauce (shoyu), only two are commonly used. Both heavy soy sauce (koikuchi shoyu) and light soy sauce (usukuchi shoyu) are used in cooking. Heavy soy sauce is the variety supplied separately at the table. Chinese soy sauce is quite sweet and should not be substituted for the Japanese variety.

Shungiku Chrysanthemum leaves used as a vegetable (see Yu dofu, page 71). They have a strong flavor, not unlike that of spinach.

Su There is no substitute for this Japanese rice vinegar, which comes in a wide variety of strengths. Look for a product with a light, sweet flavor.

Sumiso White miso thinned with vinegar and used as a dressing (see Nasu denraku, page 63).

Tonkatsu sauce Known as usuta sosu, this is a less pungent, Japanese version of Worcester sauce.

Umeboshi This dried, pickled plum is consumed daily throughout Japan as an aid to digestion. Usually red, it is eaten with rice or is rinsed or salted, even as tempura.

Wakame Familiar as the green, chewy seaweed in miso soup, highly nutritious wakame is bought dried or salted and is softened in water before use (see Wakame seaweed salad, page 57).

Wasabi Often called Japanese horseradish, green wasabi is sold in powdered form or as a paste. It normally accompanies sushi or sashimi, and is best used in moderation until you become familiar with its bite.

Su

Sumiso

Tonkatsu sauce

Umeboshi

Wakame

Wasabi

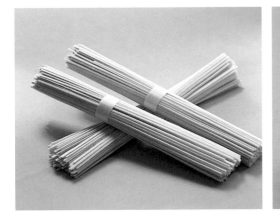

Chukasoba

Harusame

Shirataki

Soba

Somen

Udon

Chukasoba An alternate name used in western Japan for Chinese-style wheat noodles, or ramen (see Hiyashi soba, page 67).

Harusame Transparent noodles made from potato or sweet-potato flour which can be served in a hot pot (see Yosenabe, page 84) or deep-fried.

Shirataki Thin noodles made from the root of devil's tongue (konnyaku), a plant related to taro (see Mizutaki, page 92).

Soba Noodles made from buckwheat flour, often with wheat flour added. They are boiled, then served cold (see Hiyashi soba, page 67).

Somen Wheat noodles that are available dried. They are usually served cold in a summer salad (see Hiyashi soba, page 67).

Udon A wheat flour noodle available round or flat, fresh or dried.

Ingredients

5 cups (2¼ lb/1.1 kg) short-grain rice

5 cups (40 fl oz/1.25 L) water

½ cup (4 fl oz/125 ml) sake (optional)

Step-by-step basic rice

1. Put rice in a large bowl and add cold water to cover. Stir rice briskly with your hands to remove any dirt. Cover rice with your hands as you carefully drain away cloudy water. Repeat process two more times. By the third rinsing, water should be clear. (Avoid washing rice too many times, as it removes starch and nourishment and also breaks grains.)

2. Place rice in a strainer to drain. In summer, it will need about 30 minutes, in winter about 1 hour.

3. If using an electric rice maker, place rice and water in rice maker and turn on. Machine will cook rice and tell you when it is ready. If cooking rice on a stove top, place drained rice and water in a heavy-bottomed saucepan and cover with a tight-fitting lid. Bring to a boil over medium heat. Do not remove lid during cooking. When water boils, raise heat to high and boil for about 3 minutes. If the pot boils over, adjust heat. Reduce heat to medium and boil for 5 minutes. Reduce heat to low and cook for 5–10 minutes. Remove from heat and remove lid. The rice should have absorbed the water. You may wish to follow the practice of some sushi bars and add sake to the rice before removing from heat. This makes the rice puff up and adds flavor.

4. Place a cheesecloth or clean kitchen towel over saucepan, re-cover and let stand for 10–15 minutes to finish cooking.

Step-by-step sushi rice

1. Place vinegar and salt in a small saucepan over low heat and stir until salt is dissolved. Add sugar and mirin and continue to stir briskly until sugar is dissolved. Do not let mixture boil. Remove from heat when saucepan is too hot to touch.

2. Place hot rice in a wooden rice tub or a large, flat-bottomed nonmetallic bowl. Spread rice evenly over bottom of tub or bowl.

3. Add sushi vinegar slowly to rice and, using rice paddle or large flat wooden spoon, distribute evenly through rice. Do not stir the rice; instead, slice paddle or spoon through rice, then lift rice and turn.

4. Use a handheld fan to cool rice. Continue mixing and fanning until rice cools to room temperature. Rice is then ready to use. Do not refrigerate rice as it will become hard. Cover with a damp, clean kitchen towel to prevent rice from drying out until served. Sushi rice will keep for 1 day, but no longer.

Makes about 8 cups (2½ lb/1.25 kg)

Ingredients

FOR SUSHI VINEGAR

½ cup (4 fl oz/125 ml) rice vinegar

1 teaspoon salt

1 tablespoon sugar

1 teaspoon mirin

Step-by-step Sushi Rice

Ingredients

4½ cups (36 fl oz/1.1 L) water

1 piece konbu, 4 inches
(10 cm) square

2 cups (½ oz/15 g) bonito flakes

SOUPS

Dashi is the base for many Japanese soups. While instant dashi is readily available and has an excellent flavor, the preparation of dashi in the traditional manner offers a superior result. The brand of instant dashi favored most by Japanese is "Aji No Moto hond-ashi."

Dashi

Wipe surface of konbu with a damp cloth. Place in a saucepan with water and soak for approximately 2 hours. Bring saucepan with soaked konbu to a rapid simmer over high heat. After 5 minutes, check center of konbu and if it is soft, remove from pan. If it is still hard, cook a little longer, then remove. Let return to a boil. Skim any scum from surface. Remove saucepan from heat, and add a little cold water to lower temperature before adding bonito flakes. Do not stir flakes but push them to bottom of pan. Let stand for 3 minutes. Strain through cheesecloth-lined colander, into a bowl.

Clear soup, popular in Japan, is a simple and subtle soup based on dashi. Many ingredients such as seafood and vegetables can be used. The ingredients are not cooked in the soup but are placed in the bowls before the soup is added, so the soup stock remains clear. The delicate flavor goes well with sushi, but also complements other types of Japanese food.

Clear **soup**
(Osuimono)

In a saucepan, bring water, shiitake, salt and mirin to a boil. Add dashi, stir until well dissolved and remove from heat; add more dashi for a stronger flavor, less dashi for a milder flavor. Remove shiitake from soup and thinly slice then return to soup.

Place a shrimp in each bowl. Divide fish pieces, tofu cubes, enoki mushrooms, scallions and mitsuba leaves among bowls. Pour soup into each bowl and serve.

Serves 4

Ingredients

4 cups (36 fl oz/1 L) water

1 small dried shiitake mushroom

½ teaspoon salt

½ teaspoon mirin

½ teaspoon instant dashi, or to taste

4 medium-sized cooked shrimp (prawns), deveined, shells removed and tails intact

4 thinly sliced pieces of white-fleshed fish, approximately 1½ inches by ¾ inch (4 cm by 2 cm), and ¼ inch (6 mm) thick, boiled

2 oz (60 g) tofu, cut into ⅜-inch (1-cm) cubes

1 oz (30 g) enoki mushrooms

1 scallion (shallot/spring onion), thinly sliced

12 mitsuba leaves, for garnish

Ingredients

4 cups (32 fl oz/1 L) water

¼ cup (2 fl oz/60 ml) shiromiso paste

½ teaspoon instant dashi, or to taste

cubed silken tofu, as desired

2 scallions (shallots/spring onions),
thinly sliced

1 tablespoon wakame seaweed,
soaked for 2 minutes in
warm water

Basic miso **soup**

Place water in a saucepan and bring to a boil. Place miso paste in a small strainer, holding it over saucepan, and press miso through strainer with back of a wooden spoon. Discard any grainy miso left in strainer. Return soup to boil and add dashi.

Divide tofu, scallions and seaweed among individual serving bowls. Pour soup liquid into each bowl, and serve immediately.

Serves 4

Hint

Miso is a traditional soup that can be served as an accompaniment to any Japanese meal. It is usually enjoyed as a part of a traditional Japanese breakfast. Other ingredients can be added to the soup. Cooked meat, seafood or vegetables such as clams, lobster, pork, daikon, onion, eggplant (aubergine) and enoki mushrooms can be added to individual bowls just before filling with soup and serving. The amounts added depend on individual preference.

Ingredients

4 oz (125 g) salmon fillet, thickly sliced

½ teaspoon salt

4 cups (32 fl oz/1 L) water

1½ teaspoons instant dashi

4 cups (8 oz/760 g) cooked short-grain rice, heated

¼ teaspoon matcha

2 tablespoons wakame seaweed, soaked in warm water for 2 minutes

2 scallions (shallots/spring onions), thinly sliced

wasabi paste

This quick and easy lunch dish can be made with cooked rice leftover from last night's dinner. Cooked rice keeps well overnight in the refrigerator. Reheat the rice in a microwave oven, or pour boiling water over the rice and drain immediately.

Salmon rice **soup**
(Shake chazuke)

Preheat broiler (grill). Place salmon slices in a single layer in a baking dish and sprinkle with salt. Broil (grill) salmon for about 2 minutes. Turn carefully with a spatula and cook on second side until almost cooked through, about 1 minute. Remove from heat.

Meanwhile, place water in a saucepan and bring to a boil. Add dashi and stir until well dissolved. Remove from heat. Divide rice among 4 bowls, sprinkle with matcha powder and top with wakame and slices of grilled salmon. Pour soup into each bowl and garnish with slices of scallions. Accompany with wasabi.

Serves 4

Hint
Spinach leaves added to the water as it is brought to a boil make a delicious addition.

Variations

1. Salty plum rice soup (Ume chazuke)
Omit salmon. Add 1–2 tablespoons umeboshi paste or 2 or 3 umeboshi plums to each bowl before serving.

2. Snapper rice soup (Tai chazuke)
Omit salmon. Before pouring the soup over rice, place 4 oz (125 g) of thinly sliced snapper fillet on rice. Pour the soup over rice and snapper. The heat will gently cook snapper.

Angled cut

Straight cut

Paper-thin slicing of white fish

SUSHI AND SASHIMI

Many types of fish and shellfish can be enjoyed raw as sashimi and sushi. The most important aspect of sushi and sashimi is that the seafood must be fresh. To determine the freshness of whole fish, make sure fish has bloodless, sparkling, crystal-clear eyes, bright pink gills, skin with a vivid color, a pleasant sea smell, and flesh that is firm and resilient to the touch. Refrigerate fish soon after purchasing. If you have time, clean and fillet to maintain its freshness. Store in the refrigerator no longer than two days.

Sashimi and sushi are usually served with tosa shoyu sauce (see recipe page 119) and wasabi. A small amount of wasabi is mixed into the soy sauce to make a sauce for dipping.

As the Japanese say, "you eat with your eyes," so presentation is very important. Slices of fish are set against mounds of shredded daikon or carrot. Slices or wedges of lemon and shiso leaves are used as garnishes and also make delicious accompaniments. Serving platters can be decorated with leaf and flower shapes cut from thin slices of carrot, daikon or cucumber. Wasabi can be placed in a mound or formed into a leaf shape with a vein pattern etched on top using a knife.

The filleted fish can be cut in different ways. It is customary to serve one or more types of fish in groups of three or five slices, which is more pleasing to the eye than an even number of slices.

Angled cut: Start with a rectangular block of fish, about 3 inches (7.5 cm) across and 1½ inches (4 cm) thick. Measure about ½ inch (12 mm) in from the top and slice off a triangular piece to make an angled edge. Holding your knife at an angle to match the angle of the edge of the block, cut slices about ¼–½ inch (6–12 mm) thick. After all slices are cut, the remaining piece of block will be triangular.

Straight cut: Using a squared-off edge of filleted fish, cut straight down along edge to make slices ¼ inch (6 mm) thick. Slices cut from tuna need to be a little thicker than those for other fish because the flesh is likely to separate if the slices are too thin.

Paper-thin slicing of white fish: Measure about 1½ inches (4 cm) from top of block and slice off a triangular piece to make an angled edge. Cut paper-thin slices at an angle along block.

Three-part fish filleting method

For making sashimi and sushi, seek out the freshest fish possible. Find a fish market that sells sashimi-quality seafood and buy fish and shellfish in season. Before beginning to cut the fish, rinse and wipe your cutting board. Keep a bowl of water on hand to wet your knife and then wipe it, or wipe the knife occasionally with a damp, clean cloth. Use clean rubber gloves to hold the fish if necessary and always try to hold the fish by its head or tail, to avoid bruising the body.

1. Wash fish thoroughly and remove scales if necessary. Using a sharp knife, slit underside from head to tail. Remove viscera and discard. Briefly rinse cavity. Place fish on cutting board, set knife behind gills and cut off head.

2. With one hand holding fish firmly, start cutting fish from the head end to the tail along backbone, lifting fillet as you cut. Set fillet aside. Turn fish and repeat to cut the second fillet.

3. Pull out or trim away any remaining bones in fillets.

4. You should have 3 pieces: 2 fillets and 1 piece with skeleton and tail. Discard skeleton and tail.

Tuna **sashimi**
(Maguro no tataki)

Ingredients

6½ oz (200 g) sashimi-grade
   tuna fillet

2 cups (5 oz/150 g) shredded daikon,
   rinsed then soaked in iced water
   until ready to use

½ small red chili pepper, (ground)
   minced, mixed with 4 tablespoons
   finely grated daikon

2 teaspoons peeled and finely grated
   fresh ginger

1 scallion (shallot/spring onion),
   thinly sliced

pesticide-free flowers, or carrots cut
   into flower shapes, for decoration

½ cup (4 fl oz/125 ml) Tosa shoyu
   (see page 119 for recipe)

Cut tuna fillet into 1-inch (2.5-cm) thick pieces. Drain shredded daikon and divide among 4 bowls. Place mounds of tuna on daikon, then garnish with daikon-chili mixture, grated ginger and scallions. Decorate with flowers or carrot shapes. Serve with tosa shoyu, adding the grated daikon, chili, ginger and scallions from each bowl to the sauce.

Serves 4

Bonito **sashimi**
(Katsuo no tataki)

Substitute tuna with bonito fillets. Carefully thread each fillet onto a long metal skewer. Light a gas flame and turn each fillet directly over hot gas flame and quickly sear. (If gas flame is not available, prepare a fire in a grill and place fish fillets on a grill rack and quickly sear, or brown on both sides in a ridged grill pan over hight heat.) Bonito should be just seared and raw in the center. Immediately place bonito in ice water to halt the cooking process. Refrigerate for 30 minutes or until ready to use.

Remove bonito strips from skewer and cut into 1-inch (2.5-cm) cubes. Drain shredded daikon and divide among 4 bowls. Place mounds of tuna on daikon, then garnish with daikon-chili mixture, grated ginger and scallions. Decorate with flowers or carrot shapes. Serve with tosa shoyu and the grated daikon, chili, ginger and scallions added from each bowl to the sauce.

Serves 4

This thinly sliced raw fish is served with a dipping sauce different from the usual soy sauce and wasabi paste. The fish for usu-zukuri must be sliced paper-thin—so thin that it is almost transparent and the pattern on a decorative plate can be seen through it (see page 36).

Finely sliced **raw fish** (Usu-zukuri)

Measure about 1½ inches (4 cm) from top of block of fish and slice off a triangular piece to make an angled edge. Using a very sharp knife and beginning at this new cut, carefully cut paper-thin slices. Lay the slices on a round flat plate, slightly overlapping them in a circle, like the petals of a flower. On each plate, attractively arrange a mound of shredded daikon, 1 lemon slice and 1 teaspoon grated ginger, and half of daikon-chili mixture. Place scallion slices in center.

Serve with ponzu sauce.

Serves 2

(see page 119 for recipe)

Ingredients

1 piece, about 6½ oz (200 g),sashimi-grade white-fleshed fish fillet such as snapper, bream, flathead, or trevally

½ cup (1½ oz/45 g) finely shredded daikon, rinsed then soaked in iced water until ready to use, for decoration

2 lemon slices

2 teaspoons peeled and finely grated fresh ginger

¼ small red chili pepper, finely grated, mixed with 2 tablespoons finely grated daikon

1 scallion (shallot/spring onion), finely sliced

1 tablespoon Ponzu sauce (see page 119 for recipe), for dipping

Ingredients

1 sheet nori

¾ cup (3½ oz/105 g) cooked sushi rice (see page 27 for instructions)

pinch wasabi paste

½ medium, ripe avocado, cut in half lengthwise

2 strips of sashimi-grade salmon, each ⅝ inch by ⅝ inch by 3½ inches (13 mm by 13 mm by 9 cm)

Step-by-step salmon and avocado roll (Ocean maki)

1. Place 1 nori sheet on a sushi mat, about 1 inch (2.5 cm) from edge closest to you. Wet hands and place sushi rice on nori and spread out evenly, leaving a strip of nori bare along edge farthest from you. Making a slightly raised ridge next to the bare strip will help keep filling in place. With a finger, spread a thin line of wasabi evenly across center of rice.

2. Lay avocado slices over wasabi.

3. Lay salmon strips along center with avocado.

4. Lifting edge of mat closest to you, roll away from you, pressing on ingredients to keep them firm. Leave bare edge of nori free. With sushi mat covering the roll and bare strip still free, hold mat in position and press to make the roll firm.

1

2

3

4

5. Lift top of sushi mat and roll so that the bare strip of nori seals the roll. Make sure the roll is completely closed.

6. Open mat and move the roll so one end of it is flush with one edge of the mat. Roll the mat and then pat your fingers against the end of the mat to make the end straight. Repeat with other end. Press the entire roll once more with the mat to shape it into an oval, circle or square.

7. Using a very sharp knife, cut the roll in half crosswise.

8. Cut each roll in half again and then cut the quarters in half to make 8 uniform slices. Cut rolls gently so they retain their shape. Arrange on a plate and serve.

Serves 2 as a starter

5

6

7

8

Ingredients

2 sheets nori

1 cup (5 oz/150 g) cooked sushi rice
(see page 27 for instructions)

pinch of wasabi paste

4 strips of sashimi-grade tuna, each
½ inch by ¼ inch by 7 inches
(12 mm by 6 mm by 18 cm)

Tuna **rolls**
(Tekka maki)

Cut nori sheets in half lengthwise. Place 1 sheet on a sushi mat, about 1 inch (2.5 cm) from edge of mat closest to you. Wet hands and take one-fourth of sushi rice in your right hand. Gently squeeze into an oblong shape and place in center on left side of nori sheet. Using your fingers, spread rice evenly over nori, working left to right and leaving a strip of nori bare along edge farthest from you.

With a finger, spread a thin line of wasabi evenly along center of rice. Lay a tuna strip over wasabi. Holding tuna in place with your fingers, use your thumbs to lift edge of sushi mat closest to you. Roll, following directions for salmon and avocado roll (see step-by-step instructions on pages 42–43).

These rolls are usually cut into 6 pieces. Using a very sharp knife, cut each roll in half, then put the halves together side by side and cut both rolls twice to yield 6 uniform pieces.

Serves 4 as a starter

Hint
Other popular combination fillings for small seaweed rolls are cucumber and sesame seeds, avocado, sweet sushi omelette, ume boshi and salty plum, and salmon, cucumber and prawns.

Ingredients

16 jumbo shrimp (green king prawns), heads and shells removed, tails intact, deveined

1 egg

1 cup (8 fl oz/250 ml) ice-cold water

1⅓ cup (5 oz/150 g) tempura flour

vegetable oil for deep-frying

½ cup (2½ oz/75 g) all-purpose (plain) flour

2 tablespoons finely grated daikon

1 teaspoon peeled and finely grated ginger

Tempura sauce (see page 120 for recipe)

Tempura **shrimp**

Make 3 or 4 shallow cuts on underside of each shrimp and press gently with hand to flatten slightly. Be careful not to break shrimp. In a bowl, beat egg lightly. Add water continuing to beat lightly. Stir in tempura flour but do not overmix. The batter will be slightly lumpy.

Pour oil into a deep, heavy-bottomed frying pan to fill 3 inches (7.5 cm) deep. Heat oil in a frying pan until it reaches 375°F (190°C) on a deep-frying thermometer. Place all-purpose flour on a plate. Working in batches, dredge shrimp in flour, shaking off excess, then dip into tempura batter, allowing excess to drain off. Carefully lower into hot oil. When batter is just beginning to set, use chopsticks to drop a little more batter onto shrimp. Continue to cook until batter is light golden brown and shrimp are cooked through, 2–2½ minutes. Using wire skimmers, remove from oil and drain on paper towels. Arrange shrimp on 4 plates each with a small pyramid of daikon topped with grated ginger. Each diner mixes ginger and daikon into tempura sauce. Serve immediately.

Serves 4

See step-by-step instructions on pages 48–49.

TEMPURA DISHES

Step-by-step shrimp tempura

1. In a bowl, beat egg lightly. Add ice water and beat lightly.

2. Stir in tempura flour, but do not overmix. The batter will be slightly lumpy.

3. Pour oil into a deep, heavy-bottomed frying pan to fill 3 inches (7.5 cm) deep. Heat oil until it reaches 375°F (190°C) on a deep-frying thermometer, or until a small piece of bread dropped into oil sizzles and turns golden.

4. Dredge shrimp (prawn) in all-purpose (plain) flour, shaking off any excess.

1

2

3

4

5. Dip flour-coated shrimp into tempura batter, allowing excess to drip away.

6. Carefully lower shrimp into hot oil.

7. When batter is beginning to set, use chopsticks to drop a little more batter onto shrimp while it is cooking.

8. Cook until light golden brown, 2–2¹/₂ minutes. Other ingredients may take longer. Using a wire skimmer, remove shrimp from oil and drain well on paper towels. Serve with tempura sauce.

5

6

7

8

Tempura vegetables

In a bowl, beat egg lightly. Add water, continuing to beat lightly. Stir in tempura flour but do not overmix. The batter will be slightly lumpy. Pour oil into a deep, heavy-bottomed frying pan to fill 3 inches (7.5 cm) deep. Heat oil until it reaches 375°F (190°F) on a deep-frying thermometer.

Place all-purpose flour on a plate. Set onion and carrot aside. Working in batches, dredge remaining vegetables in flour, shaking off excess, then dip into tempura batter, allowing excess to drain off. Do not completely dip beans, bell peppers, snow peas and asparagus into the batter. Leaving some of these vegetables uncovered with batter is better for presentation. In a bowl, combine onion and carrot. Working in batches, dredge onion and carrot mixture in flour, shaking off excess, then dip into tempura batter, allowing excess to drain off.

Carefully lower into hot oil. Cook until light golden brown, 30 seconds–2 minutes, depending on the vegetable. Using a wire skimmer, remove from oil and drain on paper towels.

Arrange vegetables on 4 plates each with a small pyramid of daikon topped with grated ginger. Each diner mixes ginger and daikon into tempura sauce. Serve immediately.

Serves 4

Ingredients

1 egg

1 cup (8 fl oz/250 ml) ice-cold water

1⅓ cup (5 oz/150 g) tempura flour

vegetable oil for deep-frying

½ cup (2½ oz/75 g) all-purpose (plain) flour

1 large zucchini (courgette), cut into ¼-inch (6-mm) slices

1 onion, finely sliced

1 carrot, finely sliced

8 oz (250 g) snow peas (mange-tout)

1 eggplant (aubergine), sliced crosswise

1 green bell pepper (capsicum), cut into strips

8 button mushrooms

1 canned lotus root, thinly sliced

8 green beans

4 asparagus spears

1 sweet potato, sliced and parboiled

2 tablespoons finely grated daikon

1 teaspoon peeled and finely grated ginger

Tempura sauce (see page 120 for recipe)

Ingredients

1 egg

1 cup (8 fl oz/250 ml) ice-cold water

1⅓ cup (5 oz/150 g) tempura flour

vegetable oil for deep-frying

½ cup (2½ oz/75 g) all-purpose (plain) flour

8 scallops, rinsed and cut in half if large

12 pieces of white-fleshed fish fillet such as snapper, whiting or bream, about 1½ inches by 3 inches (4 cm by 7.5 cm) each

2 squid tubes, rinsed and cut in half lengthwise, then crosswise into slices about 1½ inches by 3 inches (4 cm by 7.5 cm)

4 large or 8 shucked small oysters, rinsed well

2 tablespoons finely grated daikon

1 teaspoon peeled and finely grated ginger

Tempura sauce (see page 120 for recipe)

Tempura **seafood**

In a bowl, beat egg lightly. Add water, continuing to beat lightly. Stir in tempura flour but do not overmix. The batter will be slightly lumpy. Pour oil into a deep, heavy-bottomed frying pan to fill 3 inches (7.5 cm) deep. Heat oil until it reaches 375°F (190°F) on a deep-frying thermometer. Place all-purpose flour on a plate. Working in batches, dredge seafood in flour, shaking off excess, then dip each piece into tempura batter, allowing excess to drain off. Carefully lower into hot oil. When batter is almost set, use chopsticks to drop a little more batter on each piece of seafood. Cook until batter is light golden brown and seafood is cooked through, 2–2½ minutes, depending on type of seafood. Using a wire skimmer, remove from oil and drain on paper towels.

Arrange seafood on 4 serving plates each with a pyramid of grated daikon topped with grated ginger. Each diner mixes daikon and ginger into the tempura sauce. Serve immediately.

Serves 4

Ingredients

10 oz (300 g) English (hothouse)
cucumber, thinly sliced

3½ oz (105 g) cabbage,
finely shredded

½-inch (12-mm) piece peeled
fresh ginger, cut into fine
matchstick strips

1½ teaspoons salt

sesame seeds, for garnish

Cucumber pickles (Kyuri no shiomomi)

In a bowl, gently mix all ingredients except sesame seeds. Cover with plastic wrap, pressing it down on surface of ingredients. Fill a smaller bowl with water and place on covered ingredients to apply weight. Let stand for 1 hour. Remove bowl of water. Drain liquid from cuccumber pickles, garnish with sesame seeds and serve.

Serves 4

Ingredients

1 lb (500 g) daikon

2 teaspoons salt

3 daikon leaves, blanched then
finely sliced

1¼-inch (3-cm) piece peeled fresh
ginger, finely grated

⅙ oz (5 g) bonito flakes

black sesame seeds, for garnish

soy sauce, for serving

Daikon pickles with bonito (Daikon no tosazuke)

Peel daikon and cut lengthwise into quarters. Thinly slice each quarter. Place daikon in a bowl and mix in salt. Set aside until daikon softens, 10–15 minutes. Gently squeeze daikon with your hands, drain liquid then add sliced leaves. Cover with plastic wrap, pressing it down on surface of ingredients. Fill a smaller bowl with water and place on ingredients to apply weight. Let stand for 1 hour. Remove bowl of water. Squeeze as much liquid as possible from daikon. Place daikon pickles in 4 bowls. Top with ginger and bonito flakes and sprinkle with sesame seeds. Add a little soy sauce just before serving.

Serves 4

Seaweed **salad**
(Hijiki no nimono)

Wash hijiki well in a large bowl of water. Any dust and sand will settle to bottom of bowl. Scoop hijiki from bowl and then soak in clean water for 20 minutes. Drain well. Place usuage in a bowl. Add boiling water to cover and soak for 3–4 minutes to remove some of oil. Remove from water, draining well. Cut usuage into strips 1/4 inch (6 mm) wide. Heat oil in a saucepan over high heat. Add carrot strips and stir-fry until softened, about 2 minutes. Add hijiki and stir-fry for 2 minutes. Add usuage and stir-fry for 2 minutes. Add dashi and sugar, bring to a boil then reduce heat to medium-low and simmer for 4–5 minutes. Add soy sauce and cover pan with a slightly smaller lid. Cook for 20–30 minutes over medium-low heat, stirring occasionally. Liquid should reduce by two-thirds. Serve warm or cold.

Serves 4

Ingredients

1 1/2 oz (40 g) hijiki

4 sheets usuage

boiling water

3 tablespoons vegetable oil

1/2 carrot, peeled and cut into thin matchstick strips

1 teaspoon instant dashi dissolved in 1 cup (8 fl oz/250 ml) water

1/2 cup (4 oz/125 g) sugar

1/2 cup (4 fl oz/125 ml) soy sauce

Wakame seaweed salad

Soak wakame in 1 cup (8 fl oz/250 ml) water for 5 minutes to rehydrate (it is not necessary to drain liquid). In a jar, combine nihaizu and sesame oil and shake until well combined. In a saucepan on high heat, bring bean shoots to a boil, turn off heat and strain. Place bean shoots in a bowl of cold water until cool; strain.

Divide bean shoots and wakame among 4 bowls. Arrange with cucumber slices and tomato wedges on top. Pour dressing over each salad and sprinkle with sesame seeds.

Serves 4

Ingredients

1 cup (1 oz/30 g) dried wakame

FOR DRESSING

1/2 cup (4 fl oz/125 ml) Nihaizu (see recipe page 119)

1 1/2 tablespoons Asian sesame oil

2 cups (8 oz/250 g) bean shoots

1 English (hothouse) cucumber, finely sliced on an angle

2 tomatoes, cut into wedges

sesame seeds, for garnish

Ingredients

FOR SESAME DRESSING

½ **cup (4 fl oz/125 ml) soy sauce**

½ **cup (4 oz/125 g) sugar**

¾ **cup (3½ oz/105 g) sesame seeds, toasted and ground in a mortar with a pestle**

1 **bunch spinach**

½ **teaspoon salt**

sesame seeds, for garnish

Spinach with sesame dressing
(Gomaae)

In a small saucepan over medium-high heat, bring soy sauce and sugar to a boil, stirring occasionally until sugar is completely dissolved. Remove from heat, let cool slightly, then add in ground sesame seeds, mixing well.

Cut stems from spinach and discard. Wash spinach thoroughly, immersing leaves in cold water and draining 3 times to remove all grit. Half fill a large saucepan with water, add salt and bring to a boil. Add spinach, return to a boil and cook spinach until wilted, 2–3 minutes. Drain and let cool.

Squeeze out as much water as possible from spinach leaves. Place spinach in a bowl and add ¼ cup (2 fl oz/60 ml) dressing, or more if desired. Divide spinach among 2 bowls and garnish with a sprinkling of sesame seeds. Serve at room temperature or cold.

Serves 2

Hint
This recipe makes extra dressing, which can be stored in the refrigerator for up to 6 months. It is also good with a salad of blanched asparagus and thinly sliced cucumber.

Variation

Beans with sesame dressing
Omit spinach. Trim ends from 8 oz (250 g) green beans, removing fibrous strings. Cut beans in half, place in a saucepan, add ½ teaspoon salt and water to cover. Bring to a boil then reduce heat to low and simmer for 5 minutes; drain. Place beans in a bowl, add ½ cup (4 fl oz/125 ml) sesame dressing and toss gently. Divide among 2 plates and garnish with a sprinkling of sesame seeds. Serve hot or cold.

Spinach **with** **bonito** (Ohitashi)

Ingredients

1 bunch spinach

1/2 cup (1/8 oz/31/2 g) bonito flakes

soy sauce

Cut roots from spinach and discard. Wash spinach leaves and stems thoroughly, immersing in cold water and draining 3 times to remove all grit. Half fill a large saucepan with water, add salt and bring to a boil. Add spinach, return to a boil and cook for 2–3 minutes. Drain and let cool.

Squeeze spinach tightly into a cylinder about 4 inches (10 cm) long. Cut in half and place each half, standing on end, in a shallow bowl. Scatter bonito flakes over top and drizzle over soy sauce to taste.

Serves 2

Okra with **bonito** (Okra no tosakake)

Ingredients

31/2 oz (105 g) small okra,
   stems removed

1/2 teaspoon salt

1/2 cup (1/8 oz/31/2 g) bonito flakes

Tosa shoyu (see page 119 for recipe)

Place okra in a small saucepan with water to cover. Add salt and bring to a boil. Reduce heat to low and simmer about 2 minutes—okra should retain shape and color. Remove from heat and let cool. Cut okra crosswise into slices 1/4 inch (6 mm) wide and divide among 4 plates. Top with bonito flakes and drizzle tosa shoyu to taste.

Serves 4

Variation

Tofu with bonito

Cut 1 lb (500 g) silken tofu into 4 blocks. Divide among 4 bowls. Top with pickled ginger, bonito flakes, grated ginger and scallions. Add tosa shoyu to taste.

Eggplant **with miso** (Nasu no dengaku)

With a small knife, make a shallow cut around outer edge of each eggplant slice and a large shallow X on top surface. Pour oil into a deep, heavy-bottomed frying pan to fill 3 inches (7.5 cm) deep. Heat oil until it reaches 375°F (190°C) on a deep-frying thermometer. Add eggplant and cook until well browned, about 5 minutes. Remove from oil and drain on paper towels. Arrange slices on a serving plate. Heat sumiso in a small saucepan over low heat and spoon onto eggplant. Garnish with chopped scallions and sprinkle with sesame seeds.

Serves 2

Ingredients

1 large eggplant (aubergine), cut lengthwise into slices about ³/₄ inch (2 cm) thick

vegetable oil, for deep-frying

¹/₃ cup (3 fl oz/90 ml) Sumiso sauce (see page 120 for recipe)

2 scallions (shallots/spring onions), finely chopped

sesame seeds, for garnish

Grilled **eggplant** (Yaki nasu)

Preheat broiler (grill). Broil (grill) eggplants, turning a few times, until soft, 2–3 minutes. Remove from broiler. Rinse under running cold water and quickly peel away skin. Cut into bite-sized pieces. Divide among 4 plates. Sprinkle eggplant with bonito flakes and grated ginger. Drizzle with tosa shoyu to taste.

Serves 4

Ingredients

4 small eggplants (aubergines)

¹/₂ cup (¹/₈ oz/3¹/₂ g) bonito flakes

1 tablespoon peeled and finely grated fresh ginger

Tosa shoyu (see page 119 for recipe)

Ingredients

1 tablespoon vegetable oil

1 small carrot, cut into
   matchstick strips

½ yellow (brown) onion,
   thinly sliced

¼ green bell pepper (capsicum),
   thinly sliced

10 snow peas (mange-tout), halved
   if large

6 leaves Chinese napa
   cabbage, shredded

1 cup (4 oz/125 g) bean shoots

1 teaspoon salt

1 teaspoon sugar

1 teaspoon instant dashi

1 tablespoon mirin

Stir-fried vegetables
(Yasai itame)

Preheat a wok or large frying pan over high heat until very hot,
then add oil. Add carrot and onion and stir-fry until softened, about
2 minutes. Add bell pepper and snow peas, then cabbage and bean
shoots. Stir-fry until carrot and onion are soft and snow peas and
cabbage are wilted. Add salt, sugar, dashi and mirin. Continue to
stir-fry until flavors are blended and vegetables are cooked to your
liking, about 3 minutes. Serve hot.

Serves 4

Summer **noodles**
(Hiyashi chuka)

In a small bowl, beat together eggs, salt, pepper and sugar. Heat a small frying pan with vegetable oil, add eggs and cook over medium heat, into a thin omelette. Remove from heat, let cool, then cut into thin shreds.

In a small saucepan over high heat, combine sugar and water and bring to a boil, stirring to dissolve sugar. Remove from heat and let cool. Add soy sauce, vinegar and sesame oil. Mix together well.

Divide noodles among 4 plates, mounding them in center of each plate. Top with cucumber, fish cake, pork or chicken and egg, radiating them around the plate. Place a little wakame and pickled ginger in center of noodles. Pour dressing at edge of mound in each plate. Place a little mustard along edge of each plate. Sprinkle with sesame seeds and serve.

Serves 4

Ingredients

2 eggs

pinch of salt

pinch of pepper

pinch of sugar

1 tablespoon vegetable oil

FOR DRESSING

⅓ cup (3 fl oz/90 ml) sugar

⅓ cup (3 fl oz/90 ml) water

½ cup (4 fl oz/125 ml) soy sauce

¼ cup (2 fl oz/60 ml) rice vinegar

1 tablespoon Asian sesame oil

13 oz (400 g) somen or chukasoba noodles, cooked until just tender, then drained

1 English (hothouse) cucumber, cut into matchstick strips

3 oz (90 g) cooked cold fish cake, cut into matchstick strips

5 oz (150 g) cooked pork or chicken breast, cut into matchstick strips

1 tablespoon wakame seaweed, soaked in cold water for 5 minutes, drained, then finely sliced

8 slices pickled ginger, finely sliced

hot English mustard to taste

sesame seeds, for garnish

Ingredients

5 oz (150 g) dried soba or
udon noodles

2 cups (16 fl oz/500 ml) water

¼ cup (2 fl oz/60 ml) soy sauce

¼ cup (2 fl oz/60 ml) mirin

1 teaspoon instant dashi

4 jumbo shrimp (green king
prawns), shells removed, tails left
intact, deveined

4 green beans, tops and
tails removed

2 slices of bell pepper (capsicum)

tempura batter (see pages 46–47
for recipe)

2 pinches very fine strips of nori,
for garnish

Tempura soba

Bring a saucepan of water to a boil. Add soba or udon noodles and stir to keep them from sticking together until water returns to boil. Reduce heat slightly and gently boil noodles until cooked, about 5 minutes for soba noodles, about 10 minutes for udon (taste noodles to check if cooked). Drain and rinse in cold water to stop cooking process.

Place water, soy sauce, mirin and dashi in a saucepan and bring to a boil. Remove stock from heat. Follow instructions for tempura shrimp and tempura vegetables (see recipe pages 46, 48 and 51) to cook shrimp and vegetables, draining them well on paper towels. Reheat noodles by dipping quickly in boiling water for 1 minute. Place noodles in 2 bowls and pour hot stock over noodles. Arrange tempura vegetables and shrimp on top of noodles. Garnish with nori strips.

Serves 2

Ingredients

5 oz (150 g) dried udon noodles

2 cups (16 fl oz/500 ml) water

¼ cup (2 fl oz/60 ml) soy sauce

¼ cup (2 fl oz/60 ml) mirin

1 teaspoon instant dashi

6 snow peas (mange-tout)

6 slices cooked chicken breast

4 mitsuba leaves

2 bok choy leaves, cut into 1 inch
(2.5 cm) lengths

2 eggs

1 scallion (shallot/spring onion),
thinly sliced

Udon hot pot

Bring a saucepan of water to a boil. Add noodles and stir to keep them from sticking together until water returns to boil. Reduce heat slightly and gently boil udon until cooked, about 10 minutes. Drain and rinse in cold water to stop cooking process. Place water, soy sauce, mirin and dashi in a saucepan and bring to a boil. Remove stock from heat. Divide noodles between 2 pots, add stock and bring to a boil. Divide snow peas, chicken, mitsuba leaves and bok choy between pots and bring each to a boil. To prevent eggs from breaking when they are added to pot, first break each egg into a bowl, then gently slide into simmering stock. Cover and simmer until egg is cooked, 3–4 minutes. Do not overcook, the yolk should still be soft. Remove from heat, sprinkle with scallion slices and serve.

Serves 2

Tofu **hot pot**
(Yu dofu)

This dish is usually cooked and served in the same pot or in small cast-iron pots or heat-proof casseroles. A dipping sauce is served separately.

Fill a large pot three-fourths full with water. Add instant dashi and bring to a boil. Add shungiku, cabbage and mushrooms and cook until softened, 4–5 minutes. Add tofu and heat through.

Serve with a small bowl of nihaizu or soy sauce for dipping. Serve with the daikon mixture and scallions separately, to be added to dipping sauce to taste.

Serves 4

Ingredients

1 teaspoon instant dashi

1 stem shungiku, cut to 4-inch (10-cm) lengths

2 leaves Chinese napa cabbage, sliced

3 fresh shiitake mushrooms

1 lb (500 g) tofu, cut into 2½-inch (6-cm) cubes

Nihaizu (see page 119 for recipe) or soy sauce

3 tablespoons finely grated daikon mixed with ¼ small red chili pepper, ground (minced)

scallions (shallots/spring onions), finely sliced

Fried **tofu** (Tosa dofu)

Place potato flour and bonito flakes in a blender or food processor and process to combine. Transfer to a plate. Pour oil into a deep, heavy-bottomed frying pan to fill 3 inches (7.5 cm) deep. Heat oil until it reaches 375°F (190°C) on a deep-frying thermometer. Working in batches, coat tofu well with bonito-flour mixture and then dip each piece in beaten egg. Deep-fry until golden brown, about 3 minutes, turning once to ensure pieces are browned evenly on all sides. Using a wire skimmer, remove tofu from oil and drain on paper towels.

Place 3 pieces of tofu in each serving bowl. Add ½ cup (4 fl oz/125 ml) tempura sauce to each bowl. Place 1 tablespoon grated daikon on tofu and top with a little grated ginger. Sprinkle with sliced scallions, then scatter nori strips over top and serve.

Serves 4

Ingredients

¼ cup (1½ oz/45 g) potato flour

¾ cup (¼ oz/7 g) bonito flakes

vegetable oil, for deep-frying

1 lb (500 g) firm tofu, cut into 12 pieces

2 eggs, beaten

2 cups (16 fl oz/500 ml) Tempura sauce (see page 120 for recipe)

4 tablespoons finely grated daikon

1 teaspoon peeled and very finely grated fresh ginger

2 scallions (shallots/spring onions), thinly sliced

nori, cut into very narrow strips about ¾ inch (2 cm) long and ⅛ inch (3 mm) wide

Ingredients

24 fresh oysters

½ teaspoon ground (minced) red chili pepper mixed with 2 tablespoons finely grated daikon

1 tablespoon peeled and finely grated fresh ginger

1 scallion (shallot/spring onion), thinly sliced

Ponzu sauce (see page 119 for recipe), for dipping

Oysters
Japanese style
(Nama gaki)

Shuck each oyster and discard top shell. Remove oysters from bottom shells and rinse well in salted water. Rinse out shells and divide among 4 plates. Return oysters to shells. Top each oyster with a little of chili-daikon mixture. Top with grated ginger and sliced scallions, dividing evenly. Diners can dip oysters into ponzu sauce or spoon sauce on oysters in shells.

Serves 4 as a starter

Mussels **misoyaki**

This method of cooking can be used for most types of shellfish, including oysters and scallops, as well as mussels. Be careful not to overcook the shellfish or they will dry out and toughen.

Preheat broiler (grill). Place mussels on a broiler pan. Broil (grill) until mussels are slightly brown and surface is drying out, about 5 minutes. Do not overcook. Spoon sumiso sauce on mussels and broil for 1 minute. Transfer to 4 plates and garnish with sliced scallions.

Serves 4

Ingredients

24 New Zealand green-lipped
   mussels or other large mussels,
   scrubbed and debearded

Sumiso sauce (see page 120
   for recipe)

2 scallions (shallots/spring onions),
   thinly sliced, for garnish

Pine-needle shrimp

(Ebi no matsubaage)

Make 3 or 4 shallow cuts along body of each shrimp to prevent it from curling while cooking. Sprinkle shrimp with salt. Place flour on a plate. Coat shrimp with flour. Dip into egg yolks and coat with somen. Firmly press somen onto shrimp.

Pour oil into a deep, heavy-bottomed frying pan to fill 3 inches (7.5 cm) deep. Heat oil over medium heat, until it reaches 325°F (170°C) on a deep-frying thermometer. Carefully slip shrimp into hot oil. Fry until shrimp are a light golden brown, 3–5 minutes, using chopsticks to turn shrimp so they cook evenly. Using a wire skimmer, remove shrimp from oil and drain on paper towels. Serve hot.

Serves 4 as a starter

Ingredients

8 jumbo shrimp (green king
   prawns), heads and shells
   removed, tails intact, deveined

salt

½ cup (3 oz/90 g) potato flour

2 egg yolks, beaten

½ bunch (2 oz/60 g) somen noodles,
   cut into ½ -inch (12-mm) pieces

vegetable oil, for deep-frying

Ingredients

FOR MAYONNAISE

2 egg yolks, with the thread removed

½ teaspoon salt

pinch of white pepper

½ teaspoon sugar

½ teaspoon instant dashi

½ teaspoon hot English mustard

1½ tablespoons rice vinegar

2 cups (16 fl oz/500 ml) vegetable oil, at room temperature

1 teaspoon wasabi paste

1 teaspoon soy sauce

12 shrimp (prawns), cut in half lengthwise and deveined

1 scallion (shallot/spring onion), thinly sliced

Shrimp with wasabi mayonnaise
(Ebi no wasabi yaki)

In a bowl, beat egg yolks well. Add salt, pepper, sugar, dashi, mustard and a few drops of rice vinegar and beat until yolks are almost white. Very slowly add oil to egg yolks, a few drops at a time, beating constantly, until mixture starts to form an emulsion. Slowly pour in remaining oil, adding remaining vinegar a few drops at a time.

In a bowl, combine mayonnaise, wasabi and soy sauce. Preheat broiler (grill). Place shrimp on a small baking dish and broil (grill) until almost cooked. Remove and spread liberally with wasabi mayonnaise. Broil until golden, 1–2 minutes. Transfer to 4 plates and garnish with sliced scallions.

Serves 4

Grilled squid
(Ika yaki)

Ingredients

- 1 whole squid or calamari, about 13 oz (400 g)
- 2 scallions (shallots/spring onions), thinly sliced
- 1 tablespoon peeled and finely grated fresh ginger
- soy sauce

To clean squid, remove tentacles and head from body and discard viscera. Remove beak and eye portion. It is unnecessary to remove membrane from body. Thoroughly rinse body pouch inside and out. Cut tentacles if too long. Preheat broiler (grill). Place squid on a broiler pan. Broil (grill) squid, turning once, about 4 minutes on each side. Cooking time will depend on thickness of squid. Do not overcook as squid will toughen.

Using tongs, transfer squid from broiler to a cutting board. Holding squid with tongs and using a sharp knife, cut squid into slices 1/4 inch (6 mm) thick. Place on a warm serving plate and sprinkle with grated ginger and scallions. Drizzle with soy sauce to taste.

Serves 4

Pippis steamed with sake
(Pippi sakamushi)

Ingredients

- 8 oz (250 g) pippis or clams, well scrubbed
- 2 tablespoons sake
- 1 teaspoon mirin
- 1/4 teaspoon instant dashi
- 1/2 teaspoon salt
- 2 thin slices of peeled ginger, cut into matchstick strips
- 1 scallion (shallot/spring onion), thinly sliced

Note: "Asari no sakamushi" is the traditional recipe in Japan, which uses "asari," a small clam-like shellfish that is similar to pippis.

Place pippis in a bowl with 3 cups (24 fl oz/750 ml) water and 1 1/2 tablespoons salt. Let stand overnight to remove any sand. Rinse pippis well. Place pippis, sake, mirin, dashi, salt and ginger in a heatproof bowl. Place bowl in a steamer set over boiling water and steam for 5–10 minutes. Remove steamer from heat and carefully remove bowl from steamer, placing it on a small heatproof plate. Sprinkle pippis with scallions and serve with a spoon so diners can enjoy the broth.

Serves 1

Fried **shrimp**
(Ebi furai)

Ingredients

12 jumbo shrimp (green king prawns), heads and shells removed, tails intact, deveined

salt and pepper

¼ cup (1½ oz/45 g) all-purpose (plain) flour

1 cup (4 oz/125 g) panko

2 eggs, lightly beaten

vegetable oil, for deep-frying

tonkatsu sauce or mayonnaise, for dipping

lemon wedges, for garnish

Make 3 or 4 shallow cuts along underside of each shrimp to prevent it from curling during cooking. Season shrimp lightly with salt and pepper. Place flour and panko on separate plates. Dredge each shrimp in flour, shaking off excess. Dip shrimp into eggs, letting excess drain off, and then coat with panko, pressing crumbs on firmly.

Pour oil into a deep, heavy-bottomed frying pan to fill 3 inches (7.5 cm) deep. Heat oil until it reaches 375°F (190°C) on a deep-frying thermometer. Working in batches, carefully slip shrimp into hot oil. Fry until shrimp are golden brown, 2–2½ minutes, using chopsticks to turn shrimp so they cook evenly. Using a wire skimmer, remove shrimp from oil and drain on paper towels. Divide among 4 plates and serve with tonkatsu sauce and mayonnaise for dipping sauces. Garnish with lemon wedges.

Serves 4

Deep-fried scallops (Hotate furai)

Ingredients

16 large white scallops, without coral

salt and pepper

½ cup (2½ oz/75 g) all-purpose (plain) flour

2 eggs, lightly beaten

1 cup (4 oz/125 g) panko

vegetable oil, for deep frying

tonkatsu sauce and mayonnaise, for dipping

lemon wedges, for garnish

Rinse scallops and prepare as for fried shrimp.

Grilled rainbow trout (Nijimasu no shioyaki)

Ingredients

4 rainbow trout, about 12 oz (375 g) each, cleaned, heads intact

salt

⅓ cup (3 fl oz/90 ml) Tosa shoyu sauce (see page 119 for recipe)

4 tablespoons finely grated daikon

2 teaspoons peeled and finely grated fresh ginger

Rinse fish well under running cold water. Sprinkle salt over skin and in cavity of each fish. Coat tail and eye areas well with salt, to prevent burning during cooking. Preheat broiler (grill). Place trout on broiler pan and cook until trout is half cooked, about 8 minutes. (Note: If cooking on a char grill, placing a saucepan lid over the fish will help keep in the moisture.)

Using a spatula, carefully turn trout and continue to broil until cooked through, about 7 minutes. Do not overcook. Cooking time will depend on the size and thickness of fish. To check if fish is done, make a small cut in thickest part. Transfer to plates decorated with a small pyramid of daikon topped with ginger on the side. Serve hot with a dipping sauce of tosa shoyu. Diners mix daikon and ginger from each plate into the tosa shoyu sauce to taste.

Serves 4

Hint

Most kinds of fish can be cooked using this method.

Ingredients

12 oz (375 g) white-fleshed fish fillets such as snapper or flathead

8 mussels, scrubbed and debearded

8 pippis or clams, well scrubbed

12 jumbo shrimp (green king prawns), heads and shells removed, tails intact, deveined

½ carrot, thinly sliced

5 oz (150 g) daikon, thinly sliced

6 Chinese napa cabbage leaves, thickly sliced

8 fresh shiitake mushrooms

½ bunch (6 oz/180 g) spinach

2 stems shungiku

4 scallions (shallots/spring onions), cut into 3-inch (7.5-cm) lengths

10 oz (300 g) silken tofu

4 cups (32 fl oz/1 L) boiling water

1 teaspoon instant dashi

Nihaizu sauce, for dipping (see page 119 for recipe)

8 tablespoons grated daikon, mixed with ½ red chili pepper, ground (minced)

2 scallions (shallots/spring onions), thinly sliced

2 oz (60 g) harusame, soaked in hot water for 5 minutes then drained

Seafood **hot pot**
(Yosenabe)

Arrange fish, shellfish, vegetables and tofu attractively on a large platter. This platter is placed on the table, and the ingredients are cooked at the table in a large pot on a portable burner or in an electric frying pan.

Fill pot or frying pan two-thirds full with boiling water and add instant dashi. Bring stock to a boil. When stock is boiling add firm vegetables, then gradually add seafood, fish, other vegetables, tofu and harusame in batches. Diners help themselves, retrieving vegetables, seafood and tofu from stock pot with chopsticks when cooked to their liking. Keep adding raw ingredients to stock as cooked ingredients are removed and eaten. Give each diner a small bowl of nihaizu to which daikon-chili mixture and scallions are added to taste.

Serves 4

CHICKEN DISHES

Yakitori **chicken skewers**

skewers

1 lb (500 g) boneless chicken thighs

5 thick scallions (shallots/spring onions), cut into 1-inch (2.5-cm) pieces

¼ cup (2 fl oz/60 ml) soy sauce

3 tablespoons brown sugar

1 teaspoon concentrated chicken stock

If using bamboo skewers, soak in water to cover to prevent them from burning.

Remove skin from chicken and cut meat into 1¼ -inch (3-cm) cubes.

Thread 4 or 5 chicken cubes and 3 or 4 scallion pieces onto each skewer.

In a saucepan over medium heat, combine soy sauce, sugar and stock and bring to a boil. Allow sauce to simmer for 3 minutes, stirring constantly, then remove from heat.

Preheat a broiler (grill). Brush a broiler pan with oil and lay skewers on pan. Broil (grill), turning several times, until cooked through, 8-10 minutes, depending on thickness and heat level. Make a cut in thickest part of meat to check meat is no longer pink. Brush skewers with sauce. Continue to turn over the chicken skewers and brush with the sauce over a low-medium heat for a few more minutes. Take care not to burn chicken. Remove from broiler and place on a warmed serving plate. Serve hot.

Serves 4

Ingredients

½ cup (4 fl oz/125 ml) sake

½ cup (4 fl oz/125 ml) soy sauce

¼ cup (1½ oz/45 g) peeled and finely grated fresh ginger

1 teaspoon garlic powder

1 lb (500 g) boneless chicken thighs, skin and fat removed, cut into 1½-inch (4-cm) cubes

1 cup (6 oz/180 g) potato flour

vegetable oil, for deep-frying

1 lemon, cut into 6 wedges

Marinated **crisp-fried chicken**

(Tori no karaage)

In a large bowl, combine sake, soy sauce, ginger and garlic powder and mix well. Add chicken cubes and stir to coat thoroughly with sauce. Cover with plastic wrap and marinate in refrigerator for at least 30 minutes but no longer than 1 hour. Drain chicken and discard marinade.

Pour oil into a deep, heavy-bottomed frying pan to fill 3 inches (7.5 cm) deep. Heat oil until it reaches 375°F (190°C) on a deep-frying thermometer. Place flour on a plate. Working in batches, dredge marinated chicken cubes well in flour. Carefully slip into hot oil and fry until chicken is golden brown, 3–4 minutes. Using a wire skimmer, remove chicken from oil and drain on paper towels. Place chicken on a warmed serving platter and serve with lemon wedges.

Serves 4

Teriyaki chicken

Remove skin and trim any fat from chicken breasts. Place each breast on a cutting board and pound gently with a meat mallet to flatten slightly. Place flour on a plate. Dredge chicken in flour. Heat oil in a frying pan over high heat. Add chicken and brown well on both sides, about 4 minutes total. Remove breasts from pan and place in a clean frying pan with teriyaki sauce. Bring sauce to a boil, then reduce heat to low and simmer, covered, for 5 minutes, turning chicken three times, until cooked through. Remove from pan and cut into slices 1/2 inch (12 mm) wide. Divide chicken among 4 plates with rice and top with teriyaki sauce from pan. Garnish with toasted sesame seeds, scallions and nori strips.

Serves 4

Ingredients

4 boneless chicken breasts

1/2 cup (2 1/2 oz/75 g) all-purpose (plain) flour

2 tablespoons vegetable oil

1/2 cup (4 fl oz/125 ml) Teriyaki sauce (see page 120 for recipe)

2 cups (16 oz/500 g) hot cooked rice

1 teaspoon sesame seeds, toasted

2 scallions (shallots/spring onions), thinly sliced, for garnish

nori, cut into fine strips, for garnish

Chicken donburi style (Oyako don)

Place water, soy sauce, mirin, dashi and sugar in a shallow frying pan with a tight-fitting lid. Bring to a boil, then add onion and chicken. Cover, reduce heat to low and simmer until chicken is opaque and onion is soft, 8–10 minutes. Add mitsuba and gradually pour eggs over liquid in pan. Tilt pan so eggs cover bottom. Cover and cook a little longer until eggs are almost set, about 1 minute. Remove pan from heat before eggs are completely set. To serve, place rice in individual serving bowls and top with egg, chicken and stock mixture. Garnish with chopped scallion and nori strips.

Serves 2

Ingredients

1 cup (8 fl oz/250 ml) water

5 tablespoons soy sauce

5 tablespoons mirin

1 teaspoon instant dashi

1/2 teaspoon sugar

1/2 large yellow (brown) onion, thinly sliced

8 oz (250 g) chicken thighs, skin removed, cut into bite-sized pieces

4 tablespoons chopped mitsuba

2 eggs, lightly beaten

2 cups (10 oz/300 g) steamed rice

1 scallion (shallot/spring onion), finely chopped, for garnish

nori, cut into thin strips, for garnish

Ingredients

- 1 lb (500 g) chicken breast fillets, skin removed and cut into bite-sized pieces
- 6 Chinese napa cabbage leaves, coarsely sliced
- ½ bunch (6 oz/180 g) spinach
- ½ carrot, finely sliced
- 4 scallions (shallots/spring onions), cut into 3-inch (7.5-cm) lengths
- ⅓ daikon, finely sliced
- 9 oz (280 g) silken tofu, cut into ¾-inch (2-cm) cubes
- 6 oz (180 g) shirataki noodles, cooked in boiling water for 5 minutes, then drained
- 4 cups (32 fl oz/1 L) boiling water
- 1 teaspoon instant dashi
- Nihaizu sauce (see page 119 for recipe), for dipping
- 2 oz (60 g) grated daikon mixed with ½ red chili pepper, ground (minced)
- 2 scallions (shallots/spring onions), thinly sliced

Chicken and vegetable hot pot
(Mizutaki)

Arrange chicken, vegetables, tofu and noodles attractively on a large platter. This plate is placed on the table and ingredients are cooked in a large pot on a portable burner or in an electric frying pan.

Fill pot or frying pan two-thirds full with boiling water and add instant dashi. Bring stock to a boil. When stock is boiling, add firm vegetables and chicken, then gradually add softer vegetables, noodles and tofu. Diners help themselves, retrieving ingredients and stock with chopsticks or serving spoons when cooked to their liking. Keep adding more raw ingredients to stock as more cooked items are removed. Give each diner a small bowl of nihaizu to which daikon-chili mixture and sliced scallions are added to taste. Diners dip vegetables and seafood into sauce bowl.

Serves 4

Japanese fried chicken (Chicken katsu)

Ingredients

1 lb (500 g) boneless chicken breasts

1 teaspoon salt

½ teaspoon pepper

1 teaspoon garlic powder

vegetable oil, for deep-frying

1 cup (5 oz/150 g) all-purpose (plain) flour

2 eggs, beaten

2 cups (8 oz/250 g) panko

4 wedges of lemon, for serving

tonkatsu sauce, for dipping

Remove skin and trim any fat from chicken breasts. Place on cutting board and pound gently with a meat mallet to flatten slightly. In a small bowl, combine salt, pepper and garlic powder and sprinkle over chicken. Pour oil into a deep, heavy-based frying pan to fill 3 inches (7.5 cm) deep. Heat oil until it reaches 375°F (190°F) on a deep-frying thermometer. Place flour on a plate. Dredge chicken in flour, then dip into beaten egg and then coat with panko, pressing on crumbs to make sure chicken is well coated.

Carefully slip chicken into hot oil and cook until coating is golden brown and chicken is opaque, 5–10 minutes. To check if cooked through, make a little cut in center of thickest part of a chicken breast. Remove chicken from oil and drain on paper towels. Using a sharp knife, cut into slices about ½ inch (12 mm) thick. Divide among 4 warmed plates. Serve with lemon wedges and tonkatsu sauce for dipping.

Serves 4

Ingredients

½ cup (4 oz/124 g) sugar

½ cup (4 fl oz/125 ml) soy sauce

1 teaspoon mirin

2 tablespoons chicken stock or water

1 lb (500 g) pork fillet, trimmed of sinew, cut into slices ½ inch (12 mm) thick

½ cup (2½ oz/ 75 g) peeled and finely grated fresh ginger

2 tablespoons vegetable oil

2 scallions (shallots/spring onions), thinly sliced

1 teaspoon sesame seeds, for garnish

Ginger pork
(Buta no shogayaki)

In a small saucepan over medium-high heat, combine sugar, soy sauce, mirin and stock or water and bring to a boil, stirring to dissolve sugar. Remove sauce from heat and set aside.

Dip both sides of each pork slice into grated ginger. Reserve any leftover ginger. Heat oil in a frying pan over medium-high heat. Add pork and fry, turning once until pork is no longer pink, 3–4 minutes. Add sauce to pan with any remaining grated ginger and bring to a boil. Reduce heat to low and simmer for 1 minute. Remove pork from pan and divide among 4 warmed plates. Spoon any remaining sauce from pan over slices. Garnish with sliced scallions and sprinkle with sesame seeds. Serve immediately.

Serves 4

Pork and vegetable dumplings (Gyoza)

Place cabbage in a large bowl. Add salt and mix into cabbage, squeezing it well with your hands. Salt draws excess moisture from cabbage. Drain as much as you can. Add remaining ingredients and mix until well combined.

Holding a wrapper in one hand, place 1 teaspoon filling in center of wrapper. Bring one side of wrapper to meet other side, then make 4 or 5 pleats to enclose filling into a neat bundle. It may be necessary to use a little water to help edges adhere. (Note: freeze any unwanted dumplings before cooking.)

In a nonstick frying pan over medium-high heat, heat 2 tablespoons vegetable oil. Add a few drops of sesame oil. Place dumplings closely together and cook for 1 minute. Add water to pan until it comes halfway up the sides of dumplings. Cover and cook on medium heat until all water has evaporated. Remove lid and add 2 tablespoons oil to pan and cook until bottoms are well browned.

To make dipping sauce, combine nihaizu, chili oil and scallions. Remove dumplings from pan and serve with dipping sauce.

Serves 10 as a starter

Ingredients

⅓ large cabbage, finely shredded

2 teaspoons salt

1 lb (500 g) ground (minced) pork shoulder

½ bunch (1 oz/30 g) garlic chives, finely chopped

1½ tablespoons sugar

1 tablespoon soy sauce

2 teaspoons garlic powder

1 tablespoon Asian sesame oil

2½ tablespoons peeled and grated fresh ginger

1 tablespoon sake

1 tablespoon potato flour

60 gyoza wrappers or gow gee wrappers

vegetable oil, for frying

few drops of sesame oil, for frying

FOR DIPPING SAUCE

Nihaizu (see page 119 for recipe)

chili oil

2 scallions (shallots/spring onions), thinly sliced

Ingredients

1 teaspoon salt

1 teaspoon garlic powder

½ teaspoon pepper

1 lb (500 g) pork fillet, trimmed of sinew, cut into slices ½ inch (12 mm) thick

vegetable oil, for deep-frying

1 cup (5 oz/150 g) all-purpose (plain) flour

2 eggs, beaten

2 cups (8 oz/250 g) panko

4 lemon wedges, for serving

tonkatsu sauce, for dipping

Deep-fried crumbed **pork fillet** (Tonkatsu)

In a small bowl, combine salt, garlic powder and pepper and sprinkle over pork slices.

Pour oil into a deep, heavy-bottomed frying pan to fill 3 inches (7.5 cm) deep. Heat oil until it reaches 375°F (190°C) on a deep-frying thermometer. Place flour on a plate. Working in batches, dredge pork slices in flour, shaking off excess. Dip into the beaten egg, letting excess drain away, then coat with panko, pressing crumbs on firmly. Slip pork slices into hot oil and fry until coating is golden brown and pork is no longer pink, 5–6 minutes. To check doneness, make a small cut in thickest part of pork. Using a wire skimmer, remove from oil and drain on paper towels. With a sharp knife, cut each slice into smaller slices 1 inch (2 cm) long, a more manageable size to eat with chopsticks. Divide pork among 4 plates. Place a wedge of lemon on each plate. Serve immediately with tonkatsu sauce for dipping.

Serves 4

Pork **donburi style** (Katsudon)

To make donburi sauce, in a small saucepan, bring all ingredients to a boil; immediately remove from heat.

In a small bowl, combine salt, garlic powder and pepper and sprinkle over pork. Pour oil into a deep, heavy-bottomed frying pan to fill 3 inches (7.5 cm) deep. Heat oil until it reaches 375°F (190°C) on a deep-frying thermometer. Place flour and panko on separate plates. Working in batches, dredge pork in flour, shaking off excess. Dip into beaten egg, letting excess drain away, then coat with panko, pressing on crumbs to make sure pork is well coated.

Carefully slip pork slices into hot oil and fry until golden brown, 5–6 minutes. Using a wire skimmer, remove from oil and drain on paper towels. Cut into strips ½ inch (12 mm) thick.

Place onions and donburi sauce in a small frying pan over high heat. Bring to a boil, reduce heat to medium and simmer, covered, until the onion softens, about 4 minutes. Add pork, return to a boil, then pour in lightly beaten eggs, tilting pan so eggs cover most of bottom. Cover and cook until eggs are almost set, about 1 minute. Remove pan from heat before eggs are completely set. To serve, place hot rice in a serving bowl and top with pork, egg and sauce. Sprinkle with sliced scallions and nori strips.

Serves 2

Ingredients

DONBURI SAUCE

1 cup (8 fl oz/250 ml) water

5 tablespoons soy sauce

5 tablespoons mirin

1 teaspoon instant dashi

½ teaspoon sugar

½ teaspoon salt

½ teaspoon garlic powder

¼ teaspoon pepper

2 pork fillets, 4 oz (125 g) each, trimmed of sinew, cut into slices ½ inch (12 mm) thick

vegetable oil, for deep-frying

½ cup (2½ oz/75 g) all-purpose (plain) flour

4 cups (16 oz/500 g) panko

2 eggs, beaten

½ large yellow (brown) onion, finely sliced

2 eggs, lightly beaten

2 cups (10 oz/300 g) steamed rice

2 scallions (shallots/spring onions), thinly sliced, for garnish

nori, cut into narrow strips, for garnish

Ingredients

½ lb (250 g) sashimi-quality tenderloin (eye fillet steak), trimmed of sinew

ice cold water

daikon, finely shredded, for decoration

2 lemon slices

2 teaspoons peeled and finely grated fresh ginger

2 tablespoons finely grated daikon

¼ small red chili pepper, ground (minced), and mixed with some grated daikon (above)

1 scallion (shallot/spring onion), finely chopped

Ponzu sauce (see page 119 for recipe), for dipping

Beef **sashimi**
(Gyu sashi/Gyu tataki)

Preheat a broiler (grill). Cut beef lengthwise into strips about 2 inches (5 cm) thick. Thread each strip onto a long metal skewer. Quickly sear beef in broiler, turning to brown on all sides. Meat should be still raw in center. Immediately place beef into ice water to halt the cooking process. Refrigerate for at least 30 minutes; this will make beef easier to slice.

Slice beef thinly, into slices about ⅛ inch (¼ cm) thick and arrange in a flower shape on a round flat platter. To decorate plate, place a mound of shredded daikon in center of platter along with lemon slices, grated ginger, daikon-chili mixture and chopped scallions. Serve with ponzu sauce. Ginger, daikon-chili mixture and scallions can be added to sauce to taste.

Serves 2

Note on raw beef
This is a traditional Japanese recipe. Buy fresh, best-quality beef.

Ingredients

1 lb (500 g) beef fillet, trimmed of sinew and fat

1 cup (8 fl oz/250 ml) soy sauce

1 cup (5 oz/150 g) sugar

1 teaspoon mirin

2 tablespoons chicken stock

1 scallion (shallot/spring onion), thinly sliced

Teriyaki sauce (see page 120 for recipe)

sesame seeds, toasted, for garnish

Teriyaki **beef**

Cut beef fillet into 4 uniform steaks. In a small saucepan over high heat, combine soy sauce, sugar, mirin and stock. Bring to a boil, stirring to dissolve sugar, and simmer for 1 minute. Remove from heat.

Preheat broiler (grill) and brush broiler pan with oil. Broil (grill) steaks by searing both sides quickly, then cook to your liking. Remove from broiler. With a sharp knife, cut steaks into ½ inch (12 mm) slices. Divide slices among 4 plates. Top with teriyaki sauce and sliced scallions. Sprinkle with sesame seeds.

Serves 4

Wafu steak

In a small saucepan over high heat, combine soy sauce, mirin, sake, vinegar, lemon juice, daikon and onion. Stir to mix well and bring to a boil; immediately remove sauce from heat and keep warm.

Preheat a broiler (grill) until hot and brush broiler pan with oil. Place steaks on pan and broil (grill) by searing both sides quickly, then cooking steaks to your liking. Remove from grill. With a sharp knife, cut steaks into ½ inch (12 mm) slices and divide among 4 warmed plates. Pour sauce over slices. Garnish each serving with 1 tablespoon grated daikon and a sprinkling of sliced scallions.

Serves 4

Ingredients

½ cup (4 fl oz/125 ml) soy sauce

½ cup (4 fl oz/125 ml) mirin

2 tablespoons sake

1 tablespoon rice vinegar

1 teaspoon lemon juice

5 oz (150 g) daikon, finely grated, plus 4 tablespoons for garnish

¼ medium yellow (brown) onion, finely grated

1 lb (500 g) beef fillet, trimmed of sinew, cut into 4 evenly-sized steaks

1 scallion (shallot/spring onion), thinly sliced

Stir-fried beef with sesame
(Yakiniku don)

In a bowl, combine sugar, soy sauce, sake, garlic and sesame oil. Add beef slices, mix until well combined and allow to marinate for 10 minutes. Heat a wok over high heat, add vegetable oil and stir-fry onions until soft, 2–3 minutes. Add marinated beef and continue to stir-fry until beef is cooked through, 2–3 minutes. Remove from heat.

Divide rice among 4 bowls. Spoon beef over rice, scatter sliced scallions over top and sprinkle with sesame seeds.

Serves 2

Ingredients

1½ tablespoons sugar

3 tablespoons soy sauce

1 tablespoon sake

1 tablespoon crushed garlic

1 tablespoon Asian sesame oil

8 oz (250 g) tenderloin or sirloin fillet (fillet steak or rump fillet), trimmed of fat and sinew, cut into thin slices

1 tablespoon vegetable oil

½ large yellow (brown) onion, thinly sliced

2 cups (10 oz/300 g) steamed rice

½ scallion (shallot/spring onion), thinly sliced

sesame seeds, toasted

Ingredients

FOR SAUCE

1 cup (8 fl oz/250 ml) soy sauce

1 cup (8 oz/250 g) sugar

1⅓ cups (11 fl oz/340 ml) chicken stock

1 lb (500 g) lean beef, sliced wafer thin

8 oz (250 g) shirataki noodles, cooked in boiling water for 5 minutes, drained and then rinsed in cold water

6½ oz (200 g) firm tofu, grilled and sliced

1 large yellow (brown) onion, sliced

scallions (shallots/spring onions), cut into 3 inch (7.5 cm) lengths

½ carrot, sliced

4 leaves Chinese napa cabbage, thickly sliced

8 button mushrooms

2 oz (60 g) beef suet (optional)

4 eggs, lightly beaten (optional)

Kanto-style sukiyaki

To make sauce, in a small saucepan, combine soy sauce, sugar and stock and bring to a boil, stirring to dissolve sugar; immediately remove sauce from heat.

Arrange beef slices in a flower shape on a large flat platter. Place noodles, tofu and vegetables on another large platter. Bring both platters to the table. Heat sukiyaki pot (a large, heavy, cast-iron pot) over a portable burner at the table or substitute an electric frying pan. Traditionally beef suet is used to grease the pan well before adding sauce; omit if preferred. Pour sauce into pot or frying pan. Add firm vegetables to sauce, then beef slices and softer vegetables. Lastly, add tofu, noodles and quick-cooking vegetables. Diners remove ingredients as they are done and transfer them to individual plates or bowls. The lightly beaten eggs are used for dipping. If the sauce becomes too strong, add hot water as needed.

Serves 4

Note on raw eggs
Dipping into raw eggs is traditional, but if preferred, particularly in areas where salmonella has been a problem, omit.

Variation

Kansai style sukiyaki
Same ingredients as for Kanto style sukiyaki are used, but the method of cooking them is different.

Method
Heat sukiyaki pot and rub generously with suet. When there is about 1 tablespoon fat in bottom of pot, add beef slices and sear on both sides. Push beef to one side, add sauce, vegetables, noodles and tofu and cook as desired. Serve with raw egg for dipping.

Shabu–shabu

To make sauce, in a bowl, combine all ingredients and mix until a smooth paste forms.

Arrange beef slices in a flower shape on a large flat platter. Arrange tofu, noodles and vegetables attractively on another large platter. Bring both platters to the table, where ingredients will cook in a large, shallow cast-iron pan over a portable burner, or in an electric frying pan.

Fill pan two-thirds full with water and add instant dashi. Bring stock to boil. Add firm vegetables such as daikon and carrot first. Then gradually add remaining vegetables, noodles and tofu. Dip beef slices into boiling stock separately; each diner holds meat with chopsticks and dips it in stock. Cook for only a few minutes, just long enough for its color to change. Overcooking will toughen meat. Give each diner separate bowls for the two dipping sauces. Serve with rice.

Serves 4

Ingredients

SHABUTARE – DIPPING SAUCE

½ cup (4 fl oz/125 ml) sesame paste

½ cup (4 fl oz/125 ml) white miso

2 tablespoons rice vinegar

2 tablespoons mirin

2 tablespoons soy sauce

½ cup (4 oz/125 g) sugar, dissolved in ¼ cup (2 fl oz/60 ml) boiling water

½ teaspoon garlic powder

2 or 3 drops chili oil, or more if desired

½ teaspoon Asian sesame oil

1 lb (500 g) lean beef, very thinly sliced

10 oz (300 g) silken tofu

6½ oz (200 g) shirataki noodles, cooked in boiling water for 5 minutes, then drained and rinsed in cold water

8 fresh shiitake mushrooms

6 Chinese napa cabbage leaves, thickly sliced

¼ bunch (3 oz/90 g) spinach

4 scallions (shallots/spring onions), cut into 4-inch (10-cm) lengths

1 small carrot, peeled and finely sliced

5 oz (150 g) daikon, finely sliced

1 teaspoon instant dashi

Nihaizu (see page 119 for recipe), for dipping

steamed rice, for serving

Ingredients

6 eggs

6½ oz (200 g) sugar

⅔ cup (5 fl oz/150 ml) heavy (double) cream

⅔ cup (5 fl oz/150 ml) milk

1 teaspoon vanilla extract (essence)

1 teaspoon matcha, or to taste

Matcha ice cream

In a bowl, using an electric mixer, beat eggs and sugar until well combined. Beat in cream, then add milk, vanilla and matcha. Add more or less matcha as desired. Place mixture in an ice-cream maker and freeze according to manufacturer's instructions.

Serves 4

Ingredients

4½ cups (36 fl oz/1.1 L) high-quality vanilla ice cream

1 teaspoon matcha

Green tea ice cream

Soften ice cream slightly, just enough to be able to work in the matcha.

Sprinkle matcha over ice cream. Using a large metal spoon, thoroughly incorporate matcha into ice cream. Return ice cream to freezer for about 2 hours.

Serves 6

Sweet azuki beans

Ingredients

1 cup (7 oz/220 g) dried azuki beans

1 cup (8 oz/250 g) sugar

pinch of salt

Place azuki beans in a bowl, add water to cover and soak overnight.

Drain beans and rinse well. Put beans in a heavy-bottomed saucepan and add water to cover. Bring to a boil, then drain. Return to saucepan and add water to cover beans by $\frac{1}{8}$ inch (1 cm). Bring to a boil and simmer, skimming any scum from surface. Continue to simmer until beans are soft, about 30 minutes. Add more water as necessary; do not let the beans go dry.

Add sugar, stirring to dissolve, then bring to a boil. Reduce heat to low and simmer, covered, stirring frequently, until beans thicken, at least another 30 minutes. It is very important to stir beans frequently as sugar can cause mixture to stick to bottom of the pan. Remove from heat, add pinch of salt and stir well. Let cool.

Serve sweet azuki beans with vanilla or green tea ice cream. They can also be mixed with softened vanilla ice cream and then refrozen to make azuki ice cream. Any leftover beans can be frozen for up to 6 days.

Serves 6–8

Ingredients

1 egg

1 cup (8 fl oz/250 ml) ice cold water

1⅓ cup (7 oz/220 g) tempura flour

vegetable oil, for deep-frying

4 bananas, sliced in half lengthwise

½ cup (2½ oz/75 g) all-purpose (plain) flour

2 tablespoons superfine (caster) sugar

4 scoops vanilla ice cream

Banana tempura

In a bowl, beat egg lightly. Add water and continue to beat lightly. Mix in tempura flour; do not overmix. Batter should be slightly lumpy.

Pour oil in a deep, heavy-bottomed frying pan to fill 3 inches (7.5 cm) deep. Heat oil until it reaches 375°F (190°C) on a deep-frying thermometer. Working in batches, dredge banana pieces in flour, shaking off excess, then dip in batter, allowing excess to drain away. Carefully slip bananas into hot oil. When batter is beginning to set, use chopsticks to drip a little extra batter on bananas. Cook until bananas are light golden brown, 3–4 minutes. Using a wire skimmer, remove bananas from oil and drain on paper towels. Arrange 2 pieces banana on each serving plate. Sprinkle lightly with sugar and serve with a scoop of ice cream.

Serves 4

Ingredients

¼ block kanten

1½ cups (12 fl oz/375 ml) water

scant 1 cup (6 oz/180 g) azuki beans, cooked (see page 115 for recipe)

1–1½ oz (30–45 g) sugar

pinch of salt

Red bean dessert
(Mizuyokan)

Separate strands of kanten, place in a bowl with water to cover and soak for 10 minutes. Drain and squeeze dry. Combine kanten and water in a saucepan over medium heat. Stir continuously until kanten is dissolved. Add sugar, stirring until dissolved, then add sweet azuki beans. Simmer, stirring frequently for 5 minutes. Remove from heat, add salt, then place saucepan in a bowl of cold water, stirring until mixture cools. Pour into 4 small ramekins that have been rinsed with water and refrigerate until set, about 3 hours. Turn out onto plates and serve.

Serves 4

SAUCES

Ponzu **sauce**

In a bowl, combine all ingredients and mix well. Keeps for up to 2 months in refrigerator.

Ingredients

½ **cup (4 fl oz/125 ml) daidai or lemon juice**

½ **cup (4 fl oz/125 ml) soy sauce**

½ **cup (4 fl oz/125 ml) Dashi (see page 28 for recipe)**

Tosa **shoyu**

In a saucepan over high heat, combine all ingredients and bring to a boil, stirring constantly. Remove from heat. Strain through a fine-mesh sieve into a bowl. Allow to cool before serving. Keeps well for up to 2 months in refrigerator.

Ingredients

1 **cup (8 fl oz/250 ml) soy sauce**

1 **cup (⅙ oz/5 g) bonito flakes**

¼ **cup (2 fl oz/60 ml) sake**

2 **teaspoons mirin**

Nihaizu **(soy and vinegar dipping sauce)**

In a bowl, combine all ingredients and mix well. Keeps well for up to 2 months in refrigerator.

Ingredients

½ **cup (4 fl oz/125 ml) Tosa shoyu (see above for recipe)**

½ **cup ((4 fl oz/125 ml) rice vinegar**

1 **teaspoon mirin**

Tempura **sauce**

Ingredients

1 cup (8 fl oz/250 ml) Dashi stock
(see page 28 for recipe)

¼ cup (2 fl oz/60 ml) soy sauce

¼ cup (2 fl oz/60 ml) mirin

In a saucepan over high heat, combine all ingredients and bring to a boil. Remove from heat. Let cool before serving. Keeps well for up to 3 days in refrigerator.

Sumiso **sauce**

Ingredients

¼ cup (2 fl oz/60 ml) shiromiso

2 tablespoons sugar

2 tablespoons sake

2 tablespoons water

1½ tablespoons rice vinegar

2 teaspoons hot English mustard

In a saucepan over high heat, combine all ingredients and bring to a boil, stirring frequently. Remove from heat and let cool before serving. Keeps well for up to 2 months in refrigerator.

Teriyaki **sauce**

Ingredients

1 cup (8 fl oz/250 ml) soy sauce

1 cup (7 oz/220 g) brown sugar

2 tablespoons chicken stock

1 teaspoon mirin

In a saucepan over high heat, combine all ingredients and bring to a boil. Simmer for 5 minutes, being careful not to let sauce boil over. Serve hot. Keeps well for up to 2 months in refrigerator.

Glossary

Asian sesame oil A fragrant, richly colored oil made from sesame seeds. Only small quantities of Asian sesame oil are required for flavoring.

Chili oil Vegetable oil infused with chilies to obtain their flavor and heat. Often tinged red, there are many varieties of chili oil available in both Asian markets and supermarkets. It will keep for up to 6 months at room temperature, but retains its flavor better if stored in the refrigerator.

Chinese napa cabbage Although closely related to bok choy or pak choi, Chinese cabbage or wong bok looks more like an elongated Western cabbage. It has wide, flat, fleshy stems almost white in color and very pale green wrinkly leaves packed closely into a tight head. It has a crisp texture, high water content, and a delicate, almost sweet flavor.

Eggplant (aubergine) Japanese eggplants are smaller and thinner than Italian (globe) eggplants. They are usually 6–8 inches (15–20 cm) long and about 2 inches (5 cm) in diameter, and have tender, sweet flesh. Choose firm, purple, smooth-skinned eggplants with straight stalks. Young eggplants do not require peeling.

Enoki mushrooms Also called enokitake mushrooms, these are pale colored with long thin stalks topped by tiny caps. They have a mild flavor and crunchy texture. Fresh mushrooms may be purchased in Asian markets and some supermarkets. Trim the root ends of the stalks before using.

Fish cakes Japanese fish cakes consist of fish paste (surimi) formed into small pillow shapes, then grilled or deep-fried. They are a popular accompaniment to drinks or as part of a hot pot (o-den). Available from Japanese food stores.

Garlic powder Made from dried garlic flakes which have been finely ground.

Japanese donabe An earthenware cooking pot used primarily for cooking stews or dishes that need simmering. Glazed on the inside, but left unglazed on the bottom, it is intended to sit directly on the heat or to be placed in the oven. A small hole in the lid allows steam to escape. The inside surface of the lid is usually patterned. When the food is cooked, the donabe doubles as a serving dish.

Kanten (agar) Also called agar-agar, this is a tasteless dried seaweed used as a setting agent, much like gelatine. It is available in blocks, powders or strands, from Asian supermarkets, healthfood stores and some large supermarkets.

Lotus root (renkon) From the lotus plant, this underwater root vegetable has a brown skin and white, starchy flesh with a distinct pattern of holes. When sliced, it takes on the characteristic wheel shape. Lotus root should be peeled before using. It discolors immediately when cut so place slices in water to which 1 teaspoon vinegar has been added. Fresh lotus root can be found at Asian markets.

Mitsuba Used as a herb in soups and salads, mitsuba, also known as Japanese wild chervil, is a form of parsley, which can be substituted.

The tastes, however, are not identical; the flavor of mitsuba is somewhat like that of celery.

Parboil To partially cook food, such as potatoes, by boiling it briefly in water.

Pickled ginger (gari) Ginger slices that have been pickled in salt and sweet vinegar. A delicate pink color, they are available in bottles and jars from Asian supermarkets.

Shiromiso White miso, with a pale yellow color, a sweet flavor, and a salt content that varies from 5 to 10 percent.

Shiso An aromatic herb that belongs to the same family as mint and basil, it is also known as perilla or Japanese basil. Buy fresh green leaves from Asian supermarkets. There is also a red variety more commonly found in Japanese pickles.

Tempura Flour (tenpura ko) This flour comes in many variations, but is basically a mixture of eggs, wheat flour and iced water. The ingredients are combined only lightly until a lumpy batter full of air bubbles forms. If the batter settles during food preparation, it should be replaced with a new batch.

Tofu, fresh Made from soybean milk with a smooth and creamy texture, and also known as bean curd or soybean curd. The Japanese "silken" variety is soft and extremely delicate, with a melt-in-the-mouth consistency. Chinese-style or firm tofu is often sold in small pre-cut blocks in plastic tubs of water. Fresh tofu is available in the refrigerated section of Asian markets and many supermarkets. Once opened, the tofu must be stored in the refrigerator in a sealed container, with enough water to cover it. The water should be changed daily to ensure the tofu keeps for its maximum time, which is only 2–5 days depending on the variety.

Index

Guide to weights and measures

The conversions given in the recipes in this book are approximate. Whichever system you use, remember to follow it consistently, thereby ensuring that the proportions are consistent throughout a recipe.

WEIGHTS

Imperial	Metric
⅓ oz	10 g
½ oz	15 g
¾ oz	20 g
1 oz	30 g
2 oz	60 g
3 oz	90 g
4 oz (¼ lb)	125 g
5 oz (⅓ lb)	150 g
6 oz	180 g
7 oz	220 g
8 oz (½ lb)	250 g
9 oz	280 g
10 oz	300 g
11 oz	330 g
12 oz (¾ lb)	375 g
16 oz (1 lb)	500 g
2 lb	1 kg
3 lb	1.5 kg
4 lb	2 kg

VOLUME

Imperial	Metric	Cup
1 fl oz	30 ml	
2 fl oz	60 ml	¼
3 fl oz	90 ml	⅓
4 fl oz	125 ml	½
5 fl oz	150 ml	⅔
6 fl oz	180 ml	¾
8 fl oz	250 ml	1
10 fl oz	300 ml	1¼
12 fl oz	375 ml	1½
13 fl oz	400 ml	1⅔
14 fl oz	440 ml	1¾
16 fl oz	500 ml	2
24 fl oz	750 ml	3
32 fl oz	1L	4

USEFUL CONVERSIONS

¼ teaspoon	1.25 ml
½ teaspoon	2.5 ml
1 teaspoon	5 ml
1 Australian tablespoon	20 ml (4 teaspoons)
1 UK/US tablespoon	15 ml (3 teaspoons)

Butter/Shortening

1 tablespoon	½ oz	15 g
1½ tablespoons	¾ oz	20 g
2 tablespoons	1 oz	30 g
3 tablespoons	1½ oz	45 g

OVEN TEMPERATURE GUIDE

The Celsius (°C) and Fahrenheit (°F) temperatures in this chart apply to most electric ovens. Decrease by 25°F or 10°C for a gas oven or refer to the manufacturer's temperature guide. For temperatures below 325°F (160°C), do not decrease the given temperature.

Oven description	°C	°F	Gas Mark
Cool	110	225	¼
	130	250	½
Very slow	140	275	1
	150	300	2
Slow	170	325	3
Moderate	180	350	4
	190	375	5
Moderately Hot	200	400	6
Fairly Hot	220	425	7
Hot	230	450	8
Very Hot	240	475	9
Extremely Hot	250	500	10